Praise for *The Salmon Sisters Harvest & Heritage*

"These pages are full of all that is charming, rugged, and delicious about Alaska. The Sisters' life-earned wisdom translates into a manual for a good life lived anywhere. I'm a happier person for having read this book, and I want to go to Alaska."

—BARTON SEAVER, chef and author of *The Joy of Seafood* and *American Seafood*

"Yes, there are recipes, but so much more is within these pages: wisdom, thoughtfulness, practicality, conservation, simplicity, poetry, and many of the things that you see when human beings are living a life in perfect harmony with nature. This work is pure, honest, and uplifting . . . it's likely to make you rethink your path in life for the better."

—TYLER SHARP, co-founder, CEO, and editor in chief of *Modern Huntsman*

"In a world of pretense and puffery, Claire and Emma are the real genuine deal. Seasons, harvests, friends, community—hard work and great reward—this is what living our best life in Alaska is all about. It's all here in this beautiful book."

—TOM KIZZIA, author of *Pilgrim's Wilderness* and *Cold Mountain Path*

"A beautifully photographed documentation of the coastal cuisine of Alaska's Kenai Peninsula that well understands the value of sharing and cooperation at the center of our food culture, the generations-old recipes and food preservation techniques in our kitchens, and the harvest rhythms of the place."

—JULIA O'MALLEY, food writer and author of *The Whale and the Cupcake: Stories of Subsistence, Longing, and Community in Alaska*

"The Salmon Sisters' new cookbook is a beautiful celebration of how deeply the seasonal changes of the Alaskan landscape shift and shape what you eat, when, and with whom. This collection is centered around thoughtful stewardship of the land, and how digging into the longstanding wisdom of our surrounding communities can make us better inhabitants, wherever we live. Filled with approachable, exciting recipes, vibrant photography, and attainable prompts and activities, Emma and Claire have created something truly extraordinary borne out of their rich Alaskan heritage."

—JULIE POINTER ADAMS, author and photographer of *Wabi-Sabi Welcome* and *Al Fresco*

"This book is a true celebration of Alaska, ocean stewardship, and family. I am inspired by these two women for many reasons—as I flip through this book, I experience a sense of awe and wonder at both the natural beauty of Alaska and the art, craft, and heritage of each of these stories. Learning from other women in Alaska, as well as celebrating the light coming and leaving the sky each season, encourages me to dive deeper into a sea of understanding."

—CHARLOTTE LANGLEY, chef, Scout brand founder, and tinned fish disruptor

"This second Salmon Sisters cookbook even outdoes the first fabulous one. As an Alaskan, I value not just the outstanding recipes, photographs, and graphics but the attentions to our seasonal round of harvesting and the importance of sustainability and protecting the environment. The reflections by Alaskan women on their lives within the seasons are an added and inspiring bonus."

—NANCY LORD, author of *Fishcamp* and *Early Warming*

The Salmon Sisters

Harvest & Heritage

Seasonal Recipes and Traditions that Celebrate the Alaskan Spirit

Emma Teal Laukitis and Claire Neaton

Photography by Dawn Heumann

SASQUATCH BOOKS
SEATTLE

To Alaska's land and sea,
in everlasting gratitude for
your wild gifts

CONTENTS

xiii Acknowledgment and Gratitude
xvii Celebrate the Seasons of Alaska with Us

3 Introduction to Spring

RECIPES
5 Sourdough Cinnamon Rolls
9 Smoked Salmon Scramble with Caper-Dill Cream on Toast
15 Dill Bullwhip Kelp Pickles
17 Fancy Spring Butters
24 Sautéed Fiddleheads with Pine Nuts, Lemon, and Oregano
27 Wild Nettle Gnocchi
33 Halibut Burgers with Wild Chimichurri
37 Lemony Clam Pasta with Crushed Pistachios
39 Wild Salmon Noodle Soup
43 Rhubarb-Cream–Filled Doughnuts
47 Grilled Oysters with Miso Seaweed Butter

49 Spring Equinox Feast
53 Spring Greens and Flower Salad
55 Spring Greens and Sea Salt Sourdough Focaccia
59 Mussels with Spring Onions, Sorrel, Cider, and Cream
63 Rhubarb-Mint Gin & Tonic
67 Spruce-Tip Ice Cream

TRADITIONS
7 Grow Sprouts in a Jar
10 Harvest Seaweed for Your Garden
16 Plant an Herb Garden
23 Forage Fiddleheads
26 Harvest Wild Nettles
31 Jig for a Halibut
36 Dig for Clams
42 Tap a Birch Tree
57 Make Your Own Sea Salt
64 Forage Spruce Tips

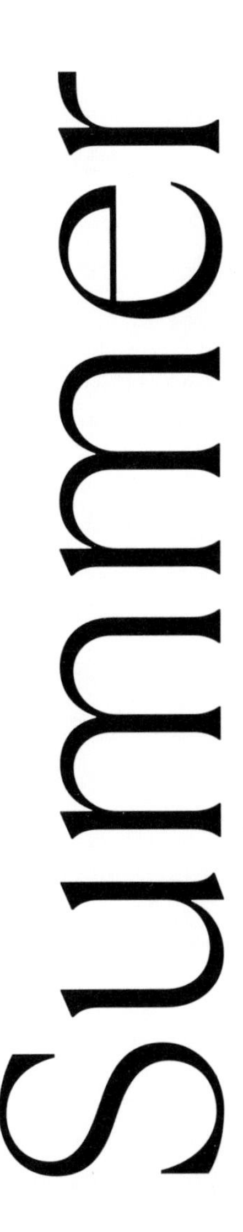

71 Introduction to Summer

RECIPES

74 Super Berry Muffins
77 Cast-Iron Baked Eggs
85 Fancy Toast with Homemade Ricotta and Salmon Caviar
91 Cured Salmon with Cucumber and Seaweed Salad in Lemony Cream Dressing
97 Tinned Octopus, Avocado, and Tomato Salad with Lime-Cilantro Dressing
98 Roasted Beets and Carrots with Anchovy-Herb Butter
99 Fried Oyster Toast
100 Tinned Salmon Niçoise Sandwich
104 Smoky Citrus, Soy, and Herb Cedar-Plank-Grilled Salmon
111 Miso Salmon and Soba Salad Bowl
117 Sea Salt Fireweed-Honey Pie

121 Summer Solstice Feast
123 Smoked Salmon Panzanella Salad
124 Fireweed (Hard) Lemonade
125 Alaska Seafood Boil
129 Lemon Olive Oil Cake with Lemony Buttercream Frosting and Blueberries

TRADITIONS

73 Pick Wild Berries
79 Celebrate the First Fish
80 Make Salmon Caviar
88 Harvest Edible Seaweed
94 Make Fish Jerky
103 Cook Fish over a Fire
107 Share Your Harvest with Your Community
113 Press Flowers
115 Make Fish Stock
116 Eat Wildflowers

Fall

133 Introduction to Fall

RECIPES

137 Crab Omelet with Wild Mushrooms, Caramelized Onion, and Brie
138 Smoked Salmon-Chive Buttermilk Biscuits
139 Pumpkin Spice Pancakes
144 Apple, Rhubarb, and Cranberry Chutney
146 Crispy Turmeric Rice with Toasted Almonds and Herbs
147 Pan-Seared Scallops with Honey-Cider Glaze
151 Tinned Salmon Carbonara with Arugula and Pine Nuts
153 Grilled Halibut Tacos with Avocado-Cilantro Crema and Pickled Onions
159 Sockeye Salmon Thai Red Curry with Chili Crisp
164 Garlic-Butter Wild Alaska Spot Prawns with Stir-Fried Noodles
165 Chocolate Peanut Butter Pie

169 Fall Equinox Feast
173 Harvest Moon Old Fashioned
175 Seafood Charcuterie Board
176 Creamy Tomato Soup with Basil Pesto
179 Black Cod with Wild Mushrooms and Kale over Creamy Grits
183 Orange and Rosemary Upside-Down Cake

TRADITIONS

134 Forage Wild Mushrooms
140 Learn the Basics of Canning
148 Quick Pickle Your Garden Vegetables
152 Harvest and Dry Herbs
156 Preserve Your Catch
161 Create Your Own Seasoning Blends
162 Gather Rose Hips
167 Make Your Own Herbal Tea

187 Introduction to Winter

RECIPES

188 Nutty Cinnamon Banana Smoothie
190 Smoked Salmon Strata with Goat Cheese and Dill
194 Creamy Steel-Cut Oats with Maple Applesauce and Walnuts
196 Crispy Smashed Potatoes with Salmon Caviar
200 Smoked Salmon Pesto Pizza
207 Fish Pie with Lemon-Dill Cream Sauce
212 Fancy Crab Mac & Cheese
215 Shrimp and Crab Gumbo
218 Salted Caramel Apple Pie

221 Winter Solstice Feast
222 Rosemary Negroni
225 Roasted Broccolini and Carrots with Tahini Dressing
226 Oyster Stew
229 Salmon Dumplings
231 Chewy Ginger Chocolate Cookies

TRADITIONS

189 Grow Bulbs Indoors
192 Stock Your Pantry with Staples
195 Light up the Night with Ice Lanterns
198 Relax and Rejuvenate in the Sauna
204 Go Ice Fishing
211 Make Winter Bird Garlands
216 Pour Homemade Candles

237 A Final Note
241 Acknowledgments
243 Index

Acknowledgment and Gratitude

We want to honor with gratitude the land and water of what has become the forty-ninth state and the Alaska Native people who have stewarded it throughout the generations, and to whom the persevering natural abundance is owed. We acknowledge the cultures of the Eyak, Tlingit, Haida, Tsimshian cultures in the southeast, the Inupiaq and St. Lawrence Island Yup'ik in the north and northwest, the Yup'ik and Cup'ik Alaska Natives in the southwest, the Athabascan people in the interior, and the Alutiiq (Sugpiaq) and Unangax̂ people of Southcentral Alaska and the Aleutian Islands, who have coexisted in balance with the land since time immemorial. Today, Native and non-Native people work together to protect these wild places that we inhabit and that sustain us, and we are committed to continuing to learn how to better take care of them for the planet and for future generations.

Celebrate the Seasons of Alaska with Us

For our Alaskan fishing family, the seasons give rhythm to life. In spring, the light returns, and along with it our energy for boat projects and preparation for the coming fishing season. We work out the winter gremlins in the engine room, start seeds in the windowsill, and swap winter boots for Xtratufs to harvest kelp, dig clams, and forage the first wild greens. Summer in Alaska is vitality and abundance, the lifeblood of our livelihood as fishermen. It's when we go to work, live at sea, trade the weekly calendar for tidal time and the marine weather forecast, and feel the most a part of our wild ecosystem. Fall gives us time to take stock and reflect after the busy summer, stow our boats and nets away, savor the harvest, and come back together with friends and family. It's a time of preservation and preparation, stocking up for the season ahead. Winter is quiet and necessary, and we're grateful for the fish and berries in our freezer to nourish us as we rest, recover, and settle into shorter, darker days in the North.

At Salmon Sisters, one of our ongoing pursuits is to inspire people to live a more meaningful and sustainable life, connected to nature and to each other. As we contemplate and witness others asking themselves how they want to live in the modern landscape, we see many acknowledging that contentment resides in the land and sea, in community, in nourishing food, in self-reliance and resourcefulness, and in the ability to stay afloat during times of change and transition. These are values ingrained in Alaskan vitality as well as in our family's lifestyle. In this book we share wisdom and traditions from our community of Alaskan women alongside recipes using ingredients that have helped people thrive in this land of extreme weather and light.

Alaskans live deeply connected to the seasons and to natural cycles of abundance. Some go to sea each summer to harvest salmon; some stay on land to plant gardens, hunt, and fish; and some leave the office on Friday afternoons and hike straight into the mountains to pick berries or the forest to forage mushrooms and wild greens. The seasons bring change, and we collectively

prepare and settle in—each fall preserving our harvest in jars or freezers to enjoy during winter, each spring planting seeds and mending our nets in preparation for summer's abundance. We share an understanding that to live well in this wild place, we must be both self-reliant and connected to our community. We must take care of our bodies, our wild home, our family and neighbors, nourishing ourselves and sharing each season's gifts, giving thanks for all Mother Nature has given us. We are made of the food we harvest from the land and sea, and in reciprocity we must steward the landscapes that support such bounty. With recipes, traditions, and stories of resilience, we offer a celebration of the Alaskan spirit and a guide for discovering capability, independence, and connection in our contemporary lives.

This book has four parts: Spring, Summer, Fall, and Winter. In each season, you'll find words to orient yourself to the time of year, stories from Alaskan women on living and eating well during this season, an illustrated guide to

seasonal traditions, and a menu meant to be prepared and shared with family and friends as a celebration of the harvest. All the recipes in each part are fresh, hearty, and simple to prepare, relying heavily on garden vegetables, Alaska seafood, and wild foods—like the dishes found in our first cookbook, *The Salmon Sisters: Feasting, Fishing, and Living in Alaska.*

We focus the stories, recipes, and imagery on self-reliance, sustainability, seasonality, connection to the natural world, and the importance of preserving Alaskan stories and food traditions. We aim to provide connection and meaning to all those who read and cook with the book, however far from Alaska you are. Celebrate each season, cook nourishing meals, and take inspiration from Alaskan resilience by harvesting and growing your own food; stay rooted in community while strengthening your self-sufficiency; keep your freezer and pantry stocked; and enjoy nature's company, embracing the natural cycles of change.

Spring
GRUNDÉNS

In Alaska, spring comes as shock and relief, easing bodies tired of skiing, hauling firewood, shoveling, and wearing heavy layers. It's a sudden reminder that quiet time is up; bid farewell to lingering cozy meals with your friends and family, begin the projects you've been pondering, finish that stack of books, and tidy up your workshop. The quiet solitude of winter with its expansive time to read, think, reflect, and create gives way to anticipation for the abundant season ahead.

With the spring equinox, we've finally made it through to the other side, and the relief is palpable on faces around town. The thawing earth yawns and stretches. Increasing daylight turns pillowy snowdrifts into crust and ice—a candied shell polished by the glinting sun rising higher in the sky each day. We start to feel the hum of chores and preparation, the momentum of awakening that will keep building at a seemingly unsustainable pace until summer bursts forward in full, unstoppable splendor.

As our families' days fill with preparation for the summer fishing season, it feels essential to sneak away from the long list of chores for a walk in the woods or on the shore to witness the first brushstrokes of spring. A brown palette mixing into greens and the company of a patch of nettles, tender young fiddleheads, a moose or bear snacking on new growth, and migrating shorebirds in the surf ground the momentum of the gaining daylight. Heading home with a basket of fresh green shoots and an awakened spirit, we feel renewed by the start of the season of wild abundance—and in this moment, we can still keep up.

In the weeks and months ahead, violets and salmonberry blossoms will bloom. Spruce tips will emerge, and blueberry bushes will bud with tiny white and pink flowers. The treasure hunt for morels will beget secrets, stories, and disappointment; halibut will be jigged up from the deep to feed families; gardens will be planted; and birch trees will be tapped for syrup for hot sourdough pancakes and the sap drunk fresh from the tree. Salmon are swimming home from the ocean toward natal rivers and streams to spawn, complete their life cycle, and create new life, bringing nutrients from the sea to the trees, plants, and animals upriver. Herring are laying eggs on kelp fronds in beautiful formations. With this energy of migration, Alaskans fall back into a rhythm with the natural world around them, grateful to have made it through another winter to appreciate the lightness of another spring.

Sourdough Cinnamon Rolls

FOR THE DOUGH:

2¾ cups all-purpose flour, plus more as needed
⅔ cup whole milk
½ cup ripe (fed) sourdough starter
2 eggs
2 tablespoons unsalted butter
2 tablespoons granulated sugar
½ teaspoon kosher salt

FOR THE FILLING:

⅔ cup packed dark brown sugar
6 tablespoons (¾ stick) unsalted butter, softened
3 teaspoons cinnamon
2 teaspoons freshly grated nutmeg
½ teaspoon allspice
2 teaspoons orange zest

FOR THE FROSTING:

½ cup confectioners' sugar, plus more for topping if desired
¼ cup unsalted butter, at room temperature
2 ounces cream cheese, at room temperature
2 teaspoons whole milk
½ teaspoon vanilla extract
Pinch of kosher salt

Imagine cinnamon rolls rising fat and fluffy in a big cast-iron pan on a sunny spot on the kitchen counter. With the oven on, the whole house becomes so warm and pleasant that you open a window. Feel the fresh spring breeze beckoning you outside to water your plants while the cinnamon rolls bake into golden-brown swirls. Come inside to make cream cheese frosting and enjoy the rolls warm and gooey out of the pan with a cup of coffee and a good view of the natural world around you.

Makes 12 cinnamon rolls

To make the dough, in the bowl of a stand mixer fitted with the dough hook attachment, add the flour, milk, sourdough starter, eggs, butter, sugar, and salt. Mix on low speed until the mixture is evenly moistened and cohesively sticky, about 3 minutes. (To make the dough by hand, beat ingredients in a large bowl about 5 minutes.) Let the dough rest for 10 minutes.

Add a little more flour to the mixture, about ⅓ cup, and mix on low speed, or beat by hand, for another 5 minutes.

Turn the dough onto a lightly floured surface and knead by hand until the dough is no longer sticky, adding a little more flour as needed while kneading. Form the dough into a smooth ball.

Place the dough in a large bowl and cover. Let the dough rest in a warm (75 degrees F) draft-free place for 4 hours. To develop strength and elasticity in the dough, give it a stretch and fold in the bowl once per hour.

To make the filling, in a medium bowl stir together the brown sugar, butter, spices, and orange zest.

To prepare the rolls for baking, turn the dough out onto a lightly floured surface and gently roll it into a 14-by-20-inch rectangle.

Spread the filling evenly onto the rectangle of dough, leaving ½ inch of exposed dough along one short edge. ⟶

Starting with the filling-coated short edge, roll the dough into a log. As you roll, the log will lengthen by several inches.

Cut the log into twelve 1½-inch slices and place them in a greased 9-by-13-inch baking pan or 10- or 12-inch cast-iron skillet. Cover the pan and let the rolls rise in a warm, draft-free spot until puffy, 2 to 3 hours.

You can let the rolls rise for another hour or so and then bake; or place the pan in the refrigerator overnight, covered, and bake the rolls the next day.

Preheat the oven to 400 degrees F.

Bake until golden, 18 to 22 minutes. (For rolls refrigerated overnight, bake for 20 to 25 minutes.) Remove the rolls from the oven and let cool for 10 to 15 minutes before frosting and serving.

To make the frosting, while the rolls are baking, in a medium bowl stir together the confectioners' sugar, butter, cream cheese, milk, vanilla, and salt until smooth.

Grow Sprouts in a Jar

SUPPLIES LIST

- cheesecloth
- rubber band
- sprouting seeds of your choosing
- wide-mouth jar

Add nutrition, flavor, and crunch to your diet with homegrown kitchen sprouts. Sprouts are essentially plant seeds that have germinated successfully and can be considered "baby" plants. There are many kinds of delicious edible sprouts, each with unique benefits and flavor. Some of our favorites include broccoli, bean, pea, alfalfa, beet, and radish sprouts, though any plant from which you would eat the stems and leaves is a good option for sprouting. We grow sprouts in the spring before the family garden has started producing, and when we're out on the boat fishing in remote places far from fresh produce for long stretches. Sprouts are easy to grow in a jar in the galley and help keep our bodies nourished and strong. Look for seeds labeled "sprouting seeds" at garden stores or in your favorite seed catalog. These will be well cleaned and pathogen-free.

Place 2 tablespoons of your chosen seeds in a jar and cover them with about 2 inches of warm water. Let the seeds soak in water overnight.

The next morning, drain the water from the jar. Secure clean cheesecloth tightly over the mouth of the jar with a rubber band. Drain the water through the cheesecloth over the sink.

Rinse the seeds by adding new water to the jar, swishing the seeds around, and draining again. Repeat the soaking, draining, and rinsing process every day until the sprouts start to turn green and grow their first leaves—this means they're ready to eat. Sprouting can take anywhere from 3 to 7 days, depending on the type of sprouts you're growing.

Store the sprouts in the refrigerator, covered, for up to a week. Enjoy them in sandwiches, salads, and rice and grain bowls, or just steal a pinch of greens every time you pass by.

Smoked Salmon Scramble with Caper-Dill Cream on Toast

We're always trying to find ways to eat fish for breakfast, and this open-faced scramble is one of our favorite morning meals. We make this on days when we have hot smoked salmon or lox on hand, good homemade sourdough or rustic bread from a local bakery, and a ripe avocado. Though the preparation is simple, this eggy, cheesy, smoky, creamy open-faced toast is truly a delight. Enjoy for a hearty breakfast, lunch, or brunch.

Makes 2 servings

FOR THE CAPER-DILL CREAM:

½ cup mayonnaise
½ cup sour cream
2 tablespoons brined capers, rinsed
2 tablespoons caper brine
1 medium lemon, first zested, then juiced
2 teaspoons finely chopped fresh dill
Hot sauce, such as Tabasco
Flaky sea salt

FOR THE EGG SCRAMBLE:

6 eggs
¼ cup whole milk or cream
Sea salt and freshly ground black pepper
1 tablespoon unsalted butter
4 to 6 ounces hot smoked salmon or lox, crumbled
2 thick slices of good-quality sourdough or rustic bread
Baby arugula or mixed greens
4 slices Brie cheese
1 ripe avocado, peeled, pitted, and sliced
Fresh dill, chopped, for garnish

To make the caper-dill cream, in a small bowl, whisk together the mayonnaise, sour cream, capers and brine, half of the lemon zest (reserve the rest for another use), lemon juice, dill, hot sauce, and salt to taste. Store in the refrigerator until the scramble is ready.

To make the egg scramble, in a medium bowl, mix the eggs and milk and season with salt and pepper. Melt the butter in a large nonstick sauté pan over medium heat. Add the egg mixture and cook until it just begins to come together, about 3 to 5 minutes, then fold in the smoked salmon. Cook for another 30 seconds and remove from heat, letting the eggs cook through.

Toast the slices of bread. Allow to cool slightly before building the open-faced sandwiches.

Divide the greens between the toast slices. Top with the Brie, then the warm egg scramble to melt the cheese, the avocado, caper-dill cream, and salt and pepper to taste. Garnish with dill.

Harvest Seaweed for Your Garden

SUPPLIES LIST

- buckets or onion sacks
- rake or flat shovel

We grew up gathering seaweed for our spring garden. Our childhood home was near the beach, so we'd head down at low tide to gather seaweed and haul it back up to our garden beds, bucket by bucket. Seaweed acts as a mulch and keeps your garden soil moist, saving water and preventing moisture from evaporating. It also eliminates the need to weed, repels slugs and other pests, enriches the soil, boosts lethargic plants, and best of all—it's free from the sea!

Along most of Alaska's coastline it's okay to harvest kelp for personal, noncommercial use without a permit if it's considered a "subsistence use area," and the kelp that's washed up on the beach is already dead; check with your regional office if you're unsure.

When out harvesting for your coastal garden, gather seaweed that's mid-beach, which is lighter to carry than the seaweed at the tide line and has fewer bugs than the seaweed up higher. Look for fine, broken-up pieces and avoid large kelp fronds that are hard to carry. Use buckets or potato or onion sacks to transport—they are lightweight, easy to grip, and let the water drain out. Be aware that seaweed patches provide food and shelter for many small marine species, so limit your impact by picking lightly from several areas rather than all in one place.

Seaweed breaks down quickly, so it's best to add it to your garden before it gets slimy—within 36 hours of gathering. Spread the seaweed thickly and evenly around garden beds, covering the soil at least 4 to 6 inches deep. The layer will shrink down as it dries. Reapply another 4- to 6-inch layer after 1 week. Once you make the second layer, the beds are usually well mulched for at least 4 to 6 weeks.

You can also save kelp to make “kelp tea,” which you can spray directly on soil or around seedlings to deter insects and pests. Just add seaweed to a bucket and fill it with water. Cover and leave this in the sun for a few days to “brew.” It has a very strong smell but is good for your garden! (It may go without saying, but this tea isn’t for drinking!)

Save some seaweed to mix into your compost or directly into the soil; trace nutrients will help condition the soil and help your garden grow. Seaweed can also be added to a garden in the fall to protect bulbs from a harsh freeze.

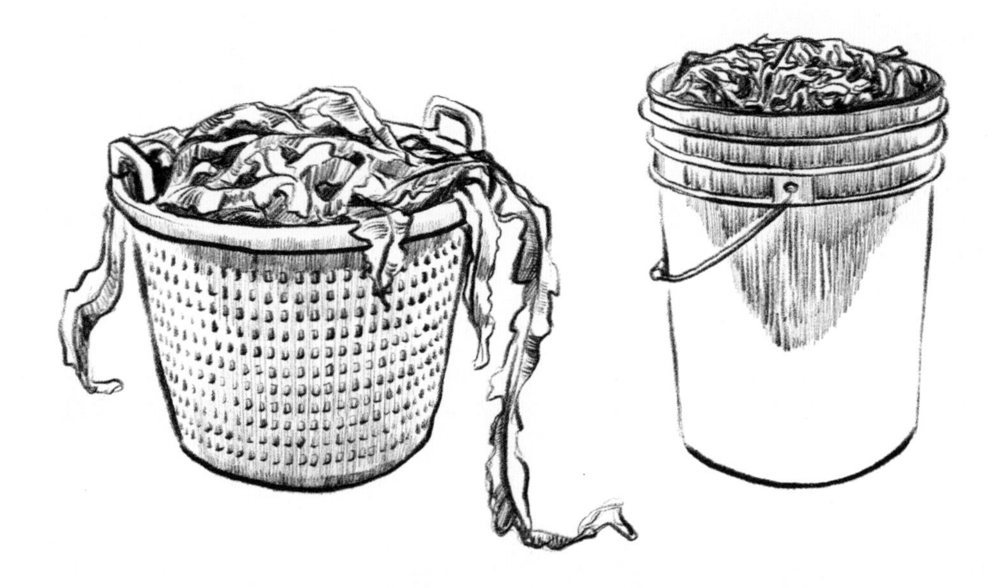

WECK

Dill Bullwhip Kelp Pickles

3 quarts bull kelp stipes
2 large white onions, sliced
¼ cup pickling salt
2 cups sugar
12 sprigs of fresh dill
2 quarts apple cider vinegar
12 cloves garlic
Cayenne peppers (optional)
3 quarts water

TOOLS NEEDED

- large pot with a lid to process the jars, filled with enough water to cover the jars by at least an inch
- small pot half-full of water to simmer the lids
- large pot to boil the pickling mixture
- colander
- clean pint or half-pint jars (keep hot in simmering water)
- ladle, spoons, canning funnel, jar grabber, rack or towels to set jars on, lid magnet, cloth to wipe rims, hot pads

Pickle your own sea vegetables! Bullwhip kelp is high in protein, dietary fiber, and nutrients, including potassium, magnesium, and iodine. Head out on a beach walk or boat ride in the spring or summer to look for kelp. Sometimes you can find it washed up on the beach after a big storm. Bring a knife and plastic bag so you can cut the choicest bits. The stipes (stalks) are the best parts to pickle. Harvest in areas that are clean and pollutant-free. Look for stipes with a smooth texture, avoiding any white spots and beaten-up edges. For the stipe, peel off the outer layer with a vegetable peeler. Pickle the kelp within a day or two of harvesting to maintain tasty freshness.

Makes 6 pint jars or 12 half-pint jars

Peel the kelp with a vegetable peeler and cut into ¼-inch rounds.

Combine the kelp and onions in a large bowl. Sprinkle with the pickling salt and stir to coat the kelp and onion. Let sit for 1 hour. Rinse well with fresh water and drain in a colander.

Add the canning jars to a large pot of water and bring to a boil. Put new, clean jar lids and rims in a small pot and cover with water; bring to a simmer.

In another large pot, combine the sugar and dill with the vinegar and bring to a boil, stirring to dissolve.

Remove a jar from the boiling water and place it on the counter. Pack the jar with kelp and onions, 1 to 2 cloves garlic (depending on the size of your jars), and a cayenne pepper. Ladle in the hot vinegar mixture, leaving a ½-inch headspace.

Wipe the rim with a clean cloth, place the lid on the jar, and screw on the ring. Repeat with the remaining jars.

Process the jars in a boiling-water bath for 10 minutes. Remove the jars from the bath and set upright on a kitchen towel to cool.

Check that all jars have sealed. Store any unsealed jars in the refrigerator and eat the pickles within a few weeks. Label the tops of the jars with a permanent marker and add to your pantry shelves. The pickles can be eaten right away, but the flavor improves after a week or two. Pickles should be enjoyed within 1 year of jarring.

Plant an Herb Garden

SUPPLIES LIST

- herb seeds
- potting soil
- a little compost (optional)
- small pots with drainage holes

Grow your own herbs and have fresh flavors at your fingertips every time you cook. Consider what herbs you use the most in your kitchen—for us, it's usually chives, rosemary, basil, mint, cilantro, parley, oregano, and sage. Having these on hand without having to make a trip to the grocery store saves time and enhances the tastiness of your cooking. Plus, growing herbs doesn't require a garden, greenhouse, or yard—they're happy to live in a few small pots in a sunny window in your kitchen.

Plant the herb seeds according to the instructions on the packet. Plant one herb variety per pot. Use good-quality potting soil and mix in a bit of compost if you have some. Herbs like full sun, so position your pots in a window that gets a lot of light. Water herbs in the mornings and in the evenings so the water doesn't evaporate immediately. Use your finger to check if you're watering enough or too much. The soil should be moist, but there shouldn't be sitting water. Your herbs should start popping their heads out of the soil in a few weeks.

Fancy Spring Butters

Spring is such an exciting time to eat in Alaska. Fresh spring delicacies make it easy to cook simply, whether your ingredients are fresh shrimp from Prince William Sound, halibut from Kodiak, sea urchins from the rocks at low tide, seaweed from the shore, or spring plants from the sunny hillsides. We find that a fancy butter is often all you need for your ingredients' natural flavors to shine. Our favorite multipurpose butters can be made in advance and used on dishes from toast to scrambled eggs, mixed into sautéed or roasted vegetables, grilled on steak, oysters, or fish, or stirred into pasta, rice, or mashed potatoes. We'll let you decide what not to use them on!

GARLIC LEMON BUTTER

Makes about ½ cup

- ½ cup (1 stick) unsalted butter, softened
- 2 tablespoons finely chopped fresh parsley
- 2 cloves garlic, minced
- 1 tablespoon freshly squeezed lemon juice
- Flaky sea salt and freshly ground black pepper
- Dash of hot sauce (optional)

In a small saucepan, melt the butter over medium heat. Add the parsley, garlic, and lemon juice. Season to taste with salt, pepper, and hot sauce. Store, covered, in the refrigerator for up to 1 week, or freeze for up to 3 months.

SEA URCHIN UNI BUTTER

Makes about ½ cup

- ½ cup (1 stick) unsalted butter, softened
- ¼ cup fresh sea urchin (uni)
- ½ teaspoon freshly squeezed lemon juice
- ½ teaspoon flaky sea salt
- Dash of hot sauce
- Fresh chives, chopped (optional)

In a small bowl, stir together the butter, uni, lemon juice, salt, and hot sauce. Sprinkle with chives. Store, covered, in the refrigerator for up to 1 week, or freeze for up to 3 months.

⟶

LEMON-ANCHOVY BUTTER

Makes about ½ cup

- ½ cup (1 stick) unsalted butter, softened
- 2 ounces anchovies in oil, minced
- 1 medium lemon, first zested, then juiced
- 2 tablespoons chopped fresh herbs (chives or tarragon)
- 1 tablespoon grated Parmesan cheese
- Flaky sea salt and freshly ground black pepper

In a small bowl, stir together the butter, anchovies with their oil, lemon zest and juice, herbs and cheese and season with salt and pepper. Whisk vigorously until thoroughly combined. Store, covered, in the refrigerator for up to 1 week, or freeze for up to 3 months.

MISO SEAWEED BUTTER

Makes about ½ cup

- 1 tablespoon dried nori or dulse
- ½ cup (1 stick) unsalted butter, softened
- 2 tablespoons white miso

In a food processor, pulse the seaweed into fine, crumb-size pieces (don't reduce it to a powder). Add the butter and miso and process until completely mixed with the nori, about 30 seconds. Store, covered, in the refrigerator for up to 1 week, or freeze for up to 3 months.

STORIES FROM ALASKAN WOMEN ON CELEBRATING SPRING

"We have an Anchors Aweigh party in the spring so we can all see each other before we disperse to different parts of Alaska to fish (an idea we stole from our friends down south). Everyone is so busy with preseason gear and boat work that we barely can talk in passing at the Gear Shed or at the harbor. Those of us who can take an afternoon and evening to hang out together on an island beach. We all arrive by boat, and the running line is full of skiffs with fishing boats on anchor. Kids make forts in the woods, hatchets are thrown into tree stumps, a bonfire is lit on the beach, and the last of the salmon fillets and moose burgers from the freezer are grilled. When the party's over, a Viking horn is blown as each family weighs anchor and motors away. Safe traveling then!"

—CATIE BURSCH, HOMER, ALASKA (DENA'INA LAND)

"Gathering with friends over outdoor bonfires as our evenings stretch later and later with growing daylight; embarking on the season's first camping trip out on a lake in late May (as the snow and ice packs allow); and preparing the garden—most recently with basil starts and transplanting rhubarb from my auntie's house."

—LINDSAY LAYLAND, DILLINGHAM, ALASKA (YUP'IK LAND)

"Spring is my favorite season. The weather is getting warmer. I start to hang my clothes out on the line and the smell of fresh sheets and blankets is grand. People in the village start setting a net out at Swedes for the first salmon. We pick wild petrushki (beach lovage) to go with our first fried fish. We start scoping out the pushki (cow parsnip) as they are getting bigger and pick the first ones that are just an inch or two high for the first taste. As the fishermen in our family are getting their boats ready and searching for parts, they are hopeful for a good fish price."

—CARLEEN HOBLET, FALSE PASS, ALASKA (UNANGAX̂ LAND)

"I celebrate the spring by eating outside as much as possible, even if that involves wearing down jackets and wool hats. When I eat outside in the fresh spring air and with the warm spring sunlight on my face, I can feel myself slowly thawing out and waking up after a long winter slumber. There's something about the first spring picnics on the beach or backyard happy hours with friends that feels extra special and celebratory after months of hearty winter meals huddled by the woodstove."

—ELIZABETH HERENDEEN, JUNEAU, ALASKA (TLINGIT LAND)

Forage Fiddleheads

We start to find the green curls of fiddlehead ferns popping up through the underbrush in early May when the snow has melted in Alaska. Even though fern plants thrive and grow large and unfurl through the summer, the young shoots are the tastiest. Fiddleheads have been considered an important spring harvest for Yup'ik, Dena'ina and Koyukon Athabascan, and Tlingit people for thousands of years. They are rich in vitamins A and C and are a popular, easily accessible wild edible full of potassium and antioxidants. Fiddleheads have a mild, earthy flavor profile similar to asparagus or spinach. They're delicious sautéed in olive oil (Sautéed Fiddleheads, page 24), made into pesto, pickled, or used as a pizza topping by many urban and rural Alaskans.

When you head out on a fiddlehead hunt, look in moist, cool areas for tight green curls covered in brown, woody, papery stuff. The tighter the curl, the tastier the fiddleheads will be. Snap off the fiddlehead with your fingers, collecting as much of the young stem as possible. (Leave the papery husk on the ferns for now.) Be careful not to pick more than a quarter of the fiddleheads per rootstock to ensure future growth.

To prepare them for cooking, remove all the papery husk with your fingers. Blanch them in boiling water to kill any bacteria that may be present on the fern heads until they start to turn a bright-green color, 4 to 5 minutes. Take the fiddleheads off the heat and place them in a bowl of ice water, gently stirring them.

To freeze fiddleheads, blanch the ferns as above, drain, and pack into sealed containers or ziplock bags.

Sautéed Fiddleheads with Pine Nuts, Lemon, and Oregano

- 2 cups freshly harvested fiddlehead ferns
- 2 tablespoons extra-virgin olive oil or unsalted butter
- 2 cloves garlic, minced
- 3 tablespoons pine nuts
- Pinch of flaky sea salt
- 1 teaspoon dried or fresh oregano
- 1 teaspoon freshly grated lemon zest
- 1 teaspoon freshly squeezed lemon juice

These tender green curls are a popular wild spring harvest (see Forage Fiddleheads, page 23) and one of our favorite sides to the first salmon of the season. They also make a tasty side to soft scrambled eggs, a crusty baguette, or a spring seafood dinner.

Makes 2 to 3 servings

Cut off the tough stems and remove any brown papery covering from the ferns. Wash them well and blot dry. Blanch, as instructed on page 23.

Heat the oil in a medium skillet over medium heat. Add the garlic and pine nuts and cook for 1 minute, stirring often. Add the fiddleheads, a sprinkle of salt, and the oregano. Sauté gently until the ferns are just tender and still vibrant green, about 5 minutes. Remove from the heat. Add the lemon zest and juice. Serve warm.

Harvest Wild Nettles

SUPPLIES LIST

- scissors
- gardening gloves
- foraging basket

Nettles are one of the first green perennials to emerge in the spring and are nutritious and surprisingly delicious to eat, despite their stinging leaves. They are rich in vitamins A, C, D, and E as well as calcium, iron, and potassium.

Watch for the buds poking up through the soil in April and May and kick off your foraging season with a pair of scissors and gloves—unless you like the bright numbing tingle of their sting! Nettles like to grow on sunny hill-sides that warm in early spring and the lower reaches of avalanche slopes in damp soil. They're best picked when they are less than 5 inches tall, and we recommend taking just the top 3 inches of the emerging plant. Nettles can be harvested all spring long; foraging for the young emerging plants is best done at higher elevations.

Nettles must be cooked to neutralize their sting, but it doesn't take much—just a light steam or sauté—similar to how you'd cook spinach or other greens. Rinse the greens to remove any grit or soil before cooking or boiling in a tea.

Wild Nettle Gnocchi

- 4 tablespoons unsalted butter, divided
- 5 ounces (about 3 heaping cups) wild nettle leaves, stemmed
- 2 eggs plus 1 egg yolk
- 10 ounces russet or Yukon gold potatoes, peeled
- 1¼ cups all-purpose flour, divided, plus more as needed
- 1 tablespoon kosher salt, plus more for seasoning
- Freshly ground black pepper
- Parmigiano Reggiano or pecorino Romano, for grating

The earthy flavor of wild nettles rolled in homemade potato gnocchi is one of the ways we love to welcome these spring delicacies into our bellies. These little green dumplings can be enjoyed with any pasta sauce or, as here, with a drizzle of melted butter and a flurry of seasonings and grated cheese. See Harvest Wild Nettles (page 26).

Makes 4 servings

Melt 2 tablespoons of the butter in a small saucepan over low heat; set aside for serving.

Melt another 2 tablespoons of the butter in a large sauté pan over medium heat. Add the nettles and cook until tender, about 5 minutes. Let them cool completely in the pan. Place the nettles on a cutting board and finely chop them. In a blender or food processor, blend the nettles, eggs, and egg yolk until a thick, cohesive paste forms, stopping occasionally to scrape down the sides with a rubber spatula.

In a medium pot, add the potatoes with enough water to cover. Bring to a simmer over medium-high heat and cook until the potatoes are tender, 15 to 20 minutes. Drain them and set aside to cool.

When the potatoes are cool enough to handle, rice or mash them in a large bowl. Add the nettle mixture and stir with a wooden spoon until well combined. Add 1 cup of flour and the salt and knead with your hands until the dough comes together. The dough should be soft but not sticky. Add more flour 1 tablespoon at a time, as needed, to achieve this texture.

Dust a work surface with the remaining ¼ cup flour, then scrape the dough from the bowl directly on top of the flour. Sprinkle the dough with additional flour to help keep it from sticking to the surface.

Line a baking sheet with parchment paper and dust with flour. Cut off a chunk of dough about 1 inch wide and cover the rest with plastic wrap. On a lightly floured work surface, use your hands to roll the chunk into a log about ½ inch in diameter. Don't add much more flour to the dough; just enough to prevent the dough from sticking to the surface. Cut the log into ½-inch pieces. Put the gnocchi on the prepared baking sheet and shape the remaining dough. Take care that the gnocchi pieces don't touch, or they will stick together. ⟶

To cook the gnocchi, bring a large pot filled with generously salted water to a boil over medium-high heat. Add the gnocchi and cook until they float to the surface, 1 to 3 minutes. Remove immediately with a slotted spoon to a serving platter or four individual bowls. Drizzle with the 2 tablespoons melted butter, a sprinkle of salt and pepper, and top with grated Parmigiano Reggiano or pecorino Romano. Serve immediately.

To store the gnocchi, refrigerate them on the baking sheet, covered with plastic wrap, for up to 2 days. Or freeze the gnocchi on the baking sheet, transfer them to an airtight container, and use within 1 month. Do not thaw before cooking.

TREASURED SPRING FOOD TRADITIONS FROM ALASKAN WOMEN

"Aside from trying to eat through everything in the freezer from the previous summer and fall, collecting freshly sprouted fiddlehead ferns and sautéing them up is a fun and tasty spring tradition, as well as trying to consume as much fresh birch water that one can handle—tapped and gifted by neighbors and friends. Also, spring goose hunting!"

—LINDSAY LAYLAND, DILLINGHAM, ALASKA (YUP'IK LAND)

"Every summer we pack our freezer full of berries, salmon, and other summer treasures. And every spring there's always a big push to clean out last summer's harvest to make room for the new. Throughout the few months of spring, we make homemade jam (rhubarb is my favorite), infuse honey and oil with herbs and spices, pickle beets and onions, can the last of the previous summer's salmon, etc. Stocking our pantry with the good, colorful food that we've harvested helps us shake off that last thought of winter and makes us feel ready for the next season ahead."

—LILY KROLL, HOMER, ALASKA (DENA'INA LAND)

Jig for a Halibut

SUPPLIES LIST

- fishing permit
- halibut pole or handline
- weighted jig
- bait (optional)
- gaff hook (optional)
- knife for bleeding
- tool for stunning, such as a wooden bat (optional)
- cooler and ice

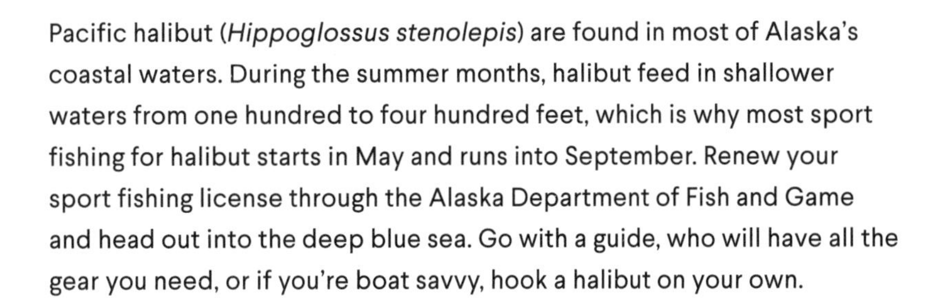

Pacific halibut (*Hippoglossus stenolepis*) are found in most of Alaska's coastal waters. During the summer months, halibut feed in shallower waters from one hundred to four hundred feet, which is why most sport fishing for halibut starts in May and runs into September. Renew your sport fishing license through the Alaska Department of Fish and Game and head out into the deep blue sea. Go with a guide, who will have all the gear you need, or if you're boat savvy, hook a halibut on your own.

Jigging for halibut is a simple and effective fishing technique that you can try while on anchor or drifting. It doesn't require bait, so you can avoid the smell and mess on deck, though sometimes we like to sweeten the deal with a piece of herring or octopus. You can rig up a halibut pole with a weighted jig or simply use a homemade handline, which can be as simple as a length of strong twine wound around a piece of wood with a weighted jig tied to one end. We grew up on boats and we always had a makeshift handline stowed away in a corner to jig for a halibut when we were on anchor.

Lower the jig until it hits the seafloor (halibut dwell at the bottom). The general idea of jigging as a catch method is to lift the jig moderately fast, then slowly drop it back down to the bottom. On the drop, the jig is fluttering or swimming, resembling a wounded fish, so this is when a halibut will likely bite. Drop your line at the same rate the jig would naturally fall, avoiding slack in the line. If you feel a bite, that's the moment to set the hook by giving your line a swift upward tug.

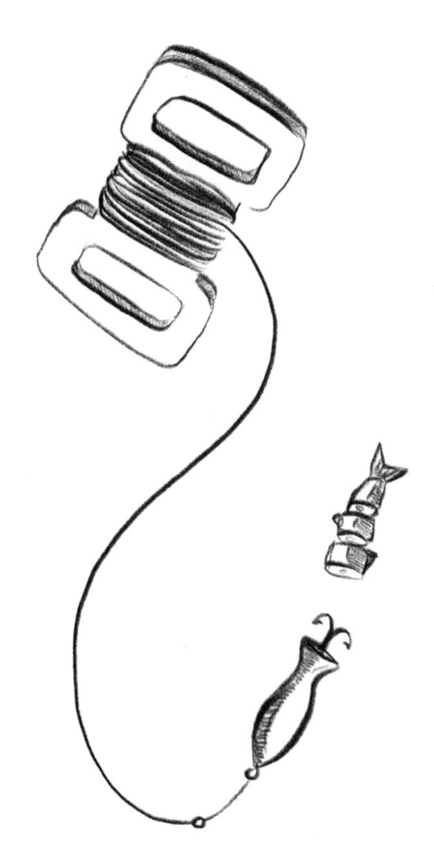

After you've set the hook, keep tension on your line by reeling in. Let out some drag if the fish wants to run. Halibut can be quite big, so be patient as you work them to the surface. Your arms may be burning, but go slow and steady, especially as you get them close to the boat. A gaff hook can be helpful for landing a large fish, but aim for the head so as not to damage any of the flesh.

Once the fish is on board, stun with a blunt wooden bat or the back of a gaff hook and bleed it immediately by sticking a sharp knife into the gills, then flip it so its white belly faces up. Slip it in a cooler packed with ice and head home to process your fish and prepare for dinner. Don't forget to cut out the halibut cheeks—they're tasty appetizers cooked up in butter!

Halibut Burgers with Wild Chimichurri

1 pound wild halibut, skin and bones removed
1 egg
2 tablespoons mayonnaise, plus more for serving
2 tablespoons Dijon mustard
½ teaspoon freshly squeezed lemon juice
¼ teaspoon cayenne, or a dash of hot sauce
1 shallot, minced
¼ cup panko bread crumbs
¼ cup fresh parsley, finely chopped
½ teaspoon garlic powder
½ teaspoon ground cumin
½ teaspoon flaky sea salt
½ teaspoon freshly ground black pepper
2 tablespoons extra-virgin olive oil
4 toasted hamburger buns or ciabatta rolls
Arugula, for topping
Avocado, sliced for topping
Fresh tomatoes, sliced for topping
Wild Chimichurri Sauce (recipe follows)

On glassy calm mornings when we were kids, our family headed out in the skiff to jig for halibut. We bundled up in coats, boots, and life jackets, packed a dry bag of snacks and a thermos of hot Tang, loaded our fishing poles, and motored out into the bay. Halibut grow large, sometimes weighing up to hundreds of pounds, so when one bit our hook, we knew exactly what it was. We reeled with all our might, and if we were lucky enough to land the fish, we had the honor of enjoying it in many delicious meals. Homemade halibut burgers with a zingy chimichurri sauce made from foraged greens is a tasty way to honor your spring catch.

Makes 4 servings

Prepare the chimichurri sauce at least an hour before serving (see page 34).

Cut the halibut into 2-inch pieces. Place pieces in a food processor and add the egg, mayonnaise, mustard, lemon juice, and cayenne. Pulse to an almost smooth consistency. Transfer mixture to a large bowl.

Add the shallot, panko, parsley, garlic powder, cumin, salt, and black pepper, and gently stir until combined.

Line a baking sheet with parchment or waxed paper so the burgers are easy to remove later. Form the mixture into four 4-inch-wide, ¾-inch-thick patties. Cover and refrigerate for at least 30 minutes or up to 12 hours ahead to help the patties bind.

Heat the oil in a large cast-iron skillet over medium-high heat or on a griddle set to 375°F. Add the patties and cook until the bottom side is browned, 4 to 5 minutes. Turn the patties and cook until the other side is browned and the patties feel firm in the center, 4 to 5 minutes. Serve immediately on a toasted bun slathered with mayonnaise and topped with fresh arugula, sliced avocado, sliced tomatoes, and a good dollop of chimichurri. ⟶

WILD CHIMICHURRI SAUCE

- 2 cloves garlic
- 1 cup fresh parsley, lightly packed
- 1 cup fresh mint, lightly packed
- 1 cup seasonal herbs and/or greens, such as sorrel, nettles, or dandelion greens
- 1 small hot chili pepper, such as serrano or jalapeño
- 3 tablespoons freshly squeezed lime juice (about 2 small limes)
- Kosher salt and freshly ground black pepper
- ⅔ cup extra-virgin olive oil

In a food processor, combine the garlic, herbs and greens, chili pepper, lime juice, and a little salt. Pulse to combine. With the motor running, drizzle in the oil. Add more salt and black pepper to taste

Alternatively, make the sauce by hand with a mortar and pestle. Pound the garlic, herbs and greens, and chili pepper to a paste. Add the lime juice, salt, and pepper, then slowly whisk in the oil.

Let sit about an hour before serving to allow the flavors to marry.

Dig for Clams

SUPPLIES LIST

- license or permit
- measuring tool
- bucket
- hand rake
- waterproof gloves
- boots or waders
- warm layers

Clam digging feels like a coastal treasure hunt and is a food-gathering activity that the whole family can enjoy together. It's also a nice way to spend time on the water and harvest seafood without needing access to a boat, expensive supplies, or calm waters.

You will need a sport fishing license or permit, depending on where you live. When you get a license, you'll learn how many clams you can dig per day and how big they must be to keep them. There are different rules and regulations for every state, so be sure you know before you go. Bring a measuring tool, a bucket, a small garden hand rake, waterproof gloves, and boots or waders. Dress warmly and expect to get pretty muddy.

Clams live in sandy, muddy, rocky areas, such as estuaries and bays. Look up popular clam-digging beaches in your area and get tips from your local marine supply stores or fish and game office. Know the tides where you want to dig; the National Oceanic and Atmospheric Administration (NOAA) releases daily tidal information. A "minus tide," when the water level is lower than usual, gives you more time on the beach as the tide stays out longer. Be careful to pay attention to the rising tide while you're digging so you don't get stuck or stranded.

Check the weather before you go. When it's colder, clams bury themselves deeper, so it's harder to dig them up. You can clam year-round, but they are often closer to the surface and easier to harvest in spring and summer.

To find clams, look for indentations and bubbles in the mud. Get down on your hands and knees and rake an inch or two below the surface until you hear or feel the rake scrape a shell. Clams group up in the same area, so if you find one, dig around for more. If you dig up a baby clam, move to another spot. Fill each hole when you're done digging and fill a bucket up with seawater for the drive home to keep the clams cool and to allow them to purge their bodies of sand and grit. Leave them in fresh seawater in the refrigerator for a few hours or overnight before steaming, shucking, and eating.

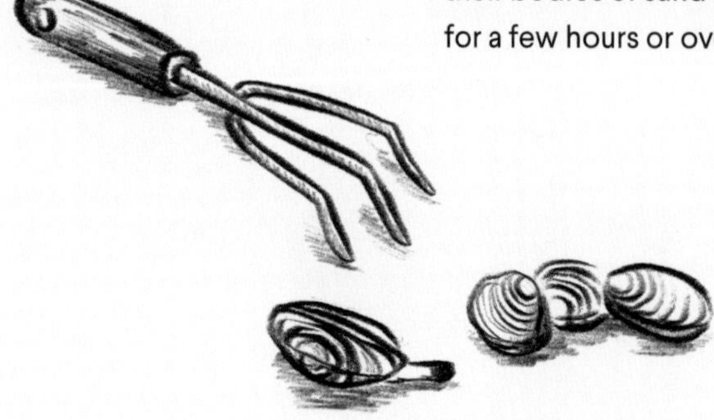

Lemony Clam Pasta with Crushed Pistachios

Kosher salt
1 pound spaghetti
2 tablespoons extra-virgin olive oil
2 cloves garlic, minced
Pinch of red pepper flakes
1½ pounds clams, scrubbed
1 cup dry white wine
1 (10.5-ounce) can white clam sauce (we like Cento brand)
2 tablespoons coarsely chopped fresh parsley, plus more for garnish
1 medium lemon, first zested, then juiced
3 tablespoons unsalted butter
Freshly ground black pepper
½ cup pistachios, crushed
Freshly grated Parmigiano Reggiano

Clams and spaghetti swirled into a bright lemon-garlic white wine sauce is one of the most perfect fresh spring meals. We live near some of the most popular clam-digging beaches in Alaska, and the best-tasting clams are harvested during favorable spring weather or early summer. Whether you're digging butter clams on a full moon, chasing after swift razor clams in the mud flats, or picking up a beautiful bag of shellfish from your local fish market, try this simple pasta recipe packed full of fresh, lemony flavor.

Makes 4 servings

Bring a large pot of water to a boil; salt generously. Add the spaghetti and cook until al dente, about 7 minutes. Drain the pasta, reserving 1 cup of the pasta water.

Meanwhile, heat the oil in a large skillet over medium heat. Add the garlic and red pepper flakes and cook until the garlic is golden, about 2 minutes. Add the clams, wine, and clam sauce and raise the heat to high. Bring to a boil, cover, and cook, shaking occasionally until all (or most) of the clams have opened, 2 to 3 minutes; discard any that remain closed. Stir in the parsley. Transfer the clam mixture to a bowl.

Return the skillet to medium-high heat. Add the reserved pasta water, lemon zest, and lemon juice; reduce the liquid until slightly thickened, about 2 minutes. Remove from the heat and whisk in the butter. Add the clam mixture and spaghetti to the skillet. Cook over medium-low heat until heated through and the pasta is coated with sauce, 2 to 3 minutes. Season with salt and pepper, and garnish with parsley, pistachios, and cheese.

Wild Salmon Noodle Soup

FOR THE BROTH:

2 tablespoons extra-virgin olive oil
1 yellow onion, peeled and halved
3 cloves garlic, smashed
5 quarter-size slices of peeled fresh ginger
1 stalk of celery, chopped
1 apple, peeled, cored, and cut into chunks
1 large carrot, peeled and chopped
1 pound napa cabbage leaves, roughly chopped
1 wild Alaska salmon head, gills removed and rinsed
1 wild Alaska salmon backbone or fillet scraps, rinsed
1 cinnamon stick
3 whole star anise
1 teaspoon coriander seeds
1 teaspoon fennel seeds
1 (10.5-ounce) can white clam juice
6 to 8 quarts water or vegetable stock
¼ cup freshly squeezed lime juice (about 2 medium limes)
¼ cup hoisin sauce
3 tablespoons soy sauce
1 tablespoon sesame oil
1 tablespoon sriracha or chili garlic paste (optional)

Salmon head soup is a staple in Alaska Native diets and is also enjoyed by many Alaskans with Scandinavian and Filipino heritage. Broth made from salmon heads and bones, cooked down to leach calcium and offer large amounts of vitamins A, C, D, E and omega-3s, was traditionally cooked by Alaska Natives to combat and prevent the cold and flu in many Southeast and Southwest Alaska communities and continues to be an important part of the gift economy in these coastal regions. Salmon head soup is cooked as medicine to share with friends and family; fishermen gift fish heads to elders, people who are susceptible to illness, or others who can't get out. Receiving fish heads, or soup made from them, means you are loved.

When the first spring salmon are running, making soup from salmon heads and bones is a great way to use up all the precious pieces of the whole fish. This pho-inspired aromatic stock is nutrient-rich, packed with warming spices, fresh herbs, and vegetables to keep your body strong and healthy through the changing seasons. If you don't have a fish head handy, try using fish bones or even fillet scraps to flavor the broth.

Makes 4 servings

To make the broth, heat the oil in a large pot over medium-high heat. Add the onion, garlic, ginger, celery, apple, carrot, and cabbage; cook, stirring constantly, 2 to 3 minutes. Chop the salmon head in half and add to the pot along with the backbone, cinnamon stick, star anise, coriander and fennel seeds, clam juice, and water or stock. Let simmer for 2 hours, adding more water as needed to keep the head and backbone submerged while cooking. Strain the broth through a fine-mesh sieve into a second large pot. Stir in the lime juice, hoisin, soy sauce, sesame oil, and sriracha. Return to a boil, then reduce the heat and simmer for 15 minutes. ⟶

FOR THE NOODLES:
1 package (8 ounces) rice vermicelli noodles

FOR THE FILLETS:
4 (3-ounce) portions wild Alaska salmon
Ground cinnamon
Kosher salt
1 tablespoon extra-virgin olive oil

FOR THE VEGETABLES:
½ yellow onion, julienned (about ½ cup)
1 carrot, julienned (about 1 cup)
½ zucchini, julienned (about 1 cup)
½ turnip, or 1 bunch radishes, julienned (about ½ cup)
1 cup thinly sliced leafy greens (such as cabbage, bok choy, or chard)

FOR THE OPTIONAL GARNISHES:
Fresh bean sprouts, Thai basil leaves, torn cilantro, jalapeño slices

Meanwhile, to prepare the noodles, place them in a large bowl. Boil enough water to cover the noodles. Soak them, covered, until soft and tender; about 7 to 10 minutes. Drain, then rinse with cold water.

To prepare the salmon, dry the fillets with paper towels, then season with the cinnamon and salt to taste. In a medium cast-iron pan, heat the oil and place the fish flesh side down in the pan. Cook until lightly browned, about 2 minutes, then flip the fillets onto the skin side and cook just until the salmon flakes and is slightly translucent at its thickest part, about 5 to 7 minutes. Remove from the heat.

Divide the broth and noodles evenly among four large bowls. Top with the vegetables and salmon. Serve with the garnishes of your choice.

Tap a Birch Tree

SUPPLIES LIST

- 7/16-inch drill bit
- handheld drill
- rubbing alcohol
- spout (from local hardware store, garden store, or online)
- hammer
- collection pail
- sap bags
- filter paper or cloth

Backyard tree tapping is a fun outdoor spring harvest that's common in Southcentral and Interior Alaska. When temperatures start to thaw, tappers head out to the birch groves to harvest sap, a rejuvenating refreshment that can be enjoyed straight from the tree or boiled into syrup. Turning sap into syrup is a time-consuming process—it takes about 110 gallons of birch sap to make 1 gallon of birch syrup! If you have the time and patience, it's a worthwhile pursuit. But for those who want to learn to tap without committing to syrup-making, drinking the fresh birch sap straight from the tree is an easy way to enjoy the birch harvest. Birch sap resembles water with a hint of sweet birch flavor—something like a cold sweet tree tea.

Head outside in mid-April and pick a birch tree that's 8 inches in diameter or larger. Be sure your tree looks healthy, with a good full crown of branches and without deadwood or fungus growth on the trunk. Look for an area on the trunk to tap that looks full or prominent, like a vein. It will often have a healthy branch above it.

Before installing the spout, sterilize it in rubbing alcohol. To install, use a drill bit that corresponds to the size of the spout. Making sure the wood you drill into is white, not brown, drill about 1½ inches into the tree at a very slight upward angle—a quick in and out. Use a stick to clear out any shavings. Tap the spout gently into the tree with a hammer. The spout needs to be tight enough to hold the weight of the sap bag or bucket full of sap, but not so tight as to split the wood around the hole.

Expect the sap to run from 14 to 21 days. On average, each tree can yield about ¾ gallon to 1 gallon of sap per day.

Harvest the sap daily and drink the hydrating spring tonic. Birch sap is very perishable but will keep in the refrigerator for several days or in the freezer forever.

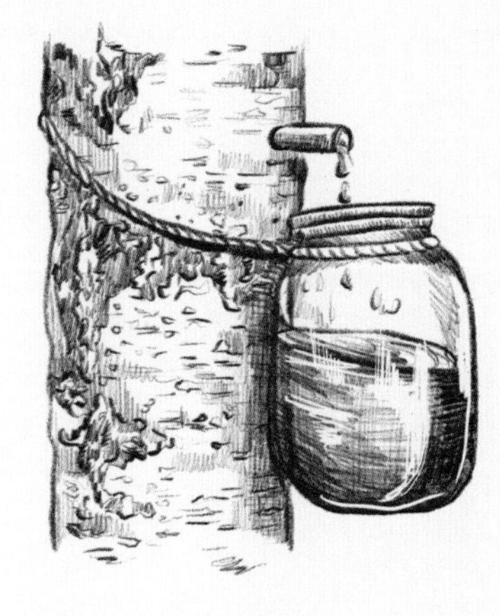

Rhubarb-Cream-Filled Doughnuts

FOR THE DOUGH:
½ cup granulated sugar
1 teaspoon kosher salt
1 cup lukewarm whole milk
1½ tablespoons active dry yeast
3½ cups all-purpose flour, plus more as needed
2 eggs, beaten
2½ tablespoons unsalted butter, melted
1 tablespoon vanilla extract

FOR THE FILLING:
3 cups sliced rhubarb
⅔ cup granulated or caster sugar
1 large lemon, first zested, then juiced
2 tablespoons cornstarch
1 teaspoon freshly grated nutmeg
2 cups vanilla yogurt

FOR FRYING:
2 cups canola oil

FOR THE TOPPING:
½ cup caster sugar
1 teaspoon ground cinnamon

Fry bread is a food fixture in many Alaska Native cultures, and we were lucky to have grown up eating it hot and sugary at potlucks and in Unangax̂ friends' kitchens in False Pass, the village near our childhood home. This doughnut recipe is inspired by our fry bread nostalgia as well as memories of fresh, sugary pastries at Mug Up in the cannery mess hall. Rhubarb grows happily in Alaska, and in spring, new ruby-red stalks ripen below huge green leaves on these perennial plants.

Makes about 16 doughnuts

To make the doughnut dough, in a large bowl, dissolve the sugar and salt in the lukewarm milk. Sprinkle in the yeast and allow to dissolve for about 10 minutes. Mix on medium speed in a stand mixer or with a hand mixer, adding the flour slowly; mix thoroughly. Add the eggs, melted butter, and vanilla and mix for another 2 minutes at the lowest speed, then at high speed for another 3 minutes.

Scrape the dough out onto a lightly floured surface and knead, adding a little additional flour at a time to keep the dough from sticking, until the dough ball is firm and only slightly tacky. Put the dough back in the large bowl and cover with a clean kitchen towel. Allow the dough to rise in a warm, draft-free place until it has doubled in size, about 2 hours.

Place the dough back to a lightly floured surface and roll it out with a rolling pin until it's about ½ inch thick. Using a round cookie cutter, doughnut cutter, or glass, cut out circles of dough and transfer them to a parchment-paper-lined baking sheet. Cover with a damp towel and let them rise for 30 to 60 minutes.

To make the filling, in a medium saucepan over medium heat, cook the rhubarb and sugar until rhubarb has softened completely, about 10 minutes. In a small bowl, mix together the lemon juice, lemon zest, cornstarch, and nutmeg and add it to the rhubarb, stirring until the mixture starts to thicken. Set aside to cool.

When the mixture has cooled, stir in the yogurt. ⟶

The doughnuts are ready to fry when the dough circles have doubled in size. Fill a Dutch oven or a large, heavy pot about one-third full with oil. Heat the oil over medium heat until a thermometer registers about 365 degrees F.

Meanwhile, in a small shallow bowl, mix the sugar and cinnamon for coating the doughnuts after frying.

When the oil has come to temperature, place 3 to 4 doughnuts in the oil and fry on one side until golden, 1 to 2 minutes. Turn with tongs and cook on the other side for another minute or two, until golden. Remove the doughnuts with a slotted spoon and drain on paper towels. Immediately roll them in the cinnamon-sugar mixture. Follow the same process for the remaining doughnuts.

To fill the doughnuts, poke a hole into each one with a chopstick. Fill a pastry filler or a plastic bag (using scissors to cut a corner) with the rhubarb mixture and pipe the filling into the center of each doughnut.

Grilled Oysters with Miso Seaweed Butter

- 2 batches Miso Seaweed Butter (see page 18)
- 2 dozen large, fresh oysters, shucked
- 1 cup cooked bacon, crumbled (optional)

We love oysters because they taste like the sea. Our home waters of Kachemak Bay grow some of the most incredible oysters we've ever tasted—sweet, salty, and plump. We slurp down the small oysters as fast as we can shuck them and save the large oysters for grilling, drizzled with this miso-seaweed butter to celebrate their ocean flavor.

Makes 2 dozen oysters

Prepare the seaweed butter according to the instructions on page 18.

To make the oysters, preheat the grill to medium heat (400 degrees F to 500 degrees F).

Place a teaspoon of the seaweed butter and a sprinkle of bacon bits on top of each oyster. Place the oysters on the grill and cook, covered, over medium-high heat until the oyster liquor starts to bubble, the butter melts, and the edge of the oysters just begin to curl, 3 to 4 minutes. Remove the oysters from the grill with tongs, transfer to a serving platter, and serve immediately.

SPRING EQUINOX FEAST

MENU

Spring Greens and Flower Salad
page 53

Spring Greens and Sea Salt Sourdough Focaccia
page 55

Mussels with Spring Onions, Sorrel, Cider, and Cream
page 59

Rhubarb-Mint Gin & Tonic
page 63

Spruce-Tip Ice Cream
page 67

Turn the page on winter and welcome in a new season of light, growth, and renewal. The spring (vernal) equinox marks the date when night and day are of about equal length all over the earth, and when in Alaska we gain more daylight than at any other time of the year. After a long winter, the first day of spring and the return of light is truly a reason to celebrate here in the North. The signs of spring may start out subtle, but it's a time to take a moment to appreciate the extra daylight, the new growth on the tips of trees and sunny hillsides, and the warmer days that lead to a wild harvest.

If the weather is fair enough, set a table outside in the late afternoon sun with a menu of fresh and foraged ingredients. Spring cooking is about appreciating the first edible plants of the season and welcoming back a new palate of flavors. Pick the first fresh shoots and young petals for a flowery salad, bake spring greens into a pan of salty, bouncy focaccia, fill a big pot with fresh mussels to cook in cider and cream. Invite friends and family to gather in celebration of the new season, toasting with a seasonal cocktail and finishing things off with a dish of homemade ice cream, the color and flavor of the awakening forest. Revel in the first taste of the season and let your feast feel uncomplicated and pure. Set up somewhere sunny, dress the table in plants and blossoms, keep warm blankets on hand, and light a fire nearby for an evening of spring delights.

Spring Greens and Flower Salad

FOR THE DRESSING:
1½ cups safflower or avocado oil
½ cup nutritional yeast
⅓ cup soy sauce
⅓ cup apple cider vinegar
⅓ cup water

FOR THE SALAD:
8 cups mixed spring greens
2 tablespoons finely chopped chives
1½ cups snap peas, thinly sliced on the bias
4 thinly sliced watermelon radishes
3 rainbow carrots, shaved into ribbons
12 edible flowers

Pansies and Johnny-jump-ups were always the first flowers to bloom in our mom's greenhouse each spring, alongside tender baby lettuces and spinach. To round out a full salad while the garden was still sparse, our mom taught us to pick young dandelion greens and sorrel leaves outside. We decorated the salad bowl with edible flower faces and a confetti of petals. There are lots of edible greens to choose from in the greenhouse and in the wild that make a lovely spring salad—try baby spinach, baby arugula, sorrel, dandelion greens, watercress, chickweed, home-grown sprouts, and pea shoots. Use edible flowers like nasturtiums, Johnny-jump-ups, pansies, tulip petals, or violets.

Makes about 6 servings

To make the dressing, combine the oil, nutritional yeast, soy sauce, vinegar, and water in a jar; cover and shake vigorously until well blended.

To make the salad, in a large bowl, add the mixed greens, then the chives, snap peas, radishes, and carrots. Toss with the dressing or dress individual servings. Arrange the edible flowers on top.

Spring Greens and Sea Salt Sourdough Focaccia

FOR THE DOUGH:

- 1½ cups ripe (fed) sourdough starter
- 1½ cups lukewarm water
- 5 cups unbleached bread flour, plus more for kneading
- 8 tablespoons extra-virgin olive oil, divided
- 2 tablespoons honey
- 1 tablespoon flaky sea salt
- 1 tablespoon instant yeast

FOR THE TOPPING:

- 2 tablespoons extra-virgin olive oil
- Fresh or dried rosemary
- Flaky sea salt
- Seasonal ingredients such as green onions, nettles, spring onions, garlic, fresh herbs, tomatoes, sorrel, or other spring greens

When spring's first greens start to emerge from the ground, we venture out to hunt for nettles, sorrel, and fireweed shoots in the evenings after all our projects are done for the day. It's exciting to see tiny green shoots coming through the forest floor, tender and new. Bake your foraged spring greens into a sourdough focaccia to enjoy with eggs in the morning, dunk into lunchtime soup or a buttery pot of clams or mussels, or serve with smoked fish and cheese. Use your best olive oil and flaky sea salt for drizzling and sprinkling on top. Start the dough the night before for an overnight rise and throw in the oven for a quick morning bake.

Makes 1 large pan of focaccia, about 12 servings

To make the dough, in a large bowl combine the sourdough starter and water. Add the flour, 6 tablespoons of the oil, the honey, salt, and yeast. Mix well, then knead until the dough is smooth and elastic, 12 to 15 minutes. (Alternatively, beat ingredients in the bowl of a stand mixer using the dough hook attachment, then knead on low speed for 5 to 7 minutes.)

Coat a large bowl lightly with olive oil and place the dough inside. Cover with a clean kitchen towel and let rise in a warm, draft-free place for 1 hour.

Gently fold the dough over five times, then let it rise again for 1 hour.

Drizzle the remaining 2 tablespoons of olive oil into the center of a 12-by-17-inch or other large-rimmed baking pan.

Transfer the dough to the pan and turn it over to coat with the oil. ⟶

With your fingers, gently stretch the dough to the edges and corners of the pan. When the dough begins to shrink back, cover and let it rest for 10 to 15 minutes to allow the dough to relax. Gently stretch the dough again, repeating the rest once more, if necessary, until the dough fills the pan.

Cover the pan and transfer it to the refrigerator to let the dough rise overnight or for up to 16 hours.

The next day, remove the pan from the refrigerator and preheat the oven to 425 degrees F.

Just before you're ready to bake, gently dimple the dough at irregular intervals with your fingertips, pressing down firmly and slowly to avoid deflating the dough.

To make the topping, drizzle the oil over the dough, enough to collect in the dimples, then sprinkle with rosemary and salt. Top with the ingredients of your choice.

Bake until the focaccia is light golden brown, 20 to 25 minutes. Slice into pieces and enjoy warm.

Make Your Own Sea Salt

SUPPLIES LIST

- food-grade 5-gallon bucket or clean milk jugs
- large baking pans
- cheesecloth
- tape
- medium sieve
- jars or salt cellars

It's easy to make your own sea salt—the ocean is filled with it! It's a fun way to taste the flavors of the local coastline, know where your salt comes from, and—bonus—it's free.

Go down to a stretch of clean, unpolluted coastline with a 5-gallon bucket, milk jugs, or other large collection container. In general, 5 gallons of seawater will produce around 5 cups of salt. Fill the container with seawater and take it home to pour into large glass baking pans. Cover the pans with thick cheesecloth and tape the edges to seal.

Set the pans near a heat source like a wood fireplace or radiator. Better yet, let Mother Nature do the work for you and leave the pans in the sun to dehydrate for 1 to 3 days, depending on the weather. Once the moisture is evaporated, loosen the salt by scraping gently with a wooden spoon or spatula.

Strain the salt through a medium sieve to remove any rocks, seaweed, or shells.

Bottle up your salt in your favorite jars and shakers, add your own label, and name the salt after your local coastline. Let your imagination play and create your own infused salts by adding herbs, spices, and other ingredients—think rosemary, edible flowers, tea leaves, citrus peel, chili peppers, dried mushrooms, dehydrated vegetables, or spruce tips. A general recipe is 1 teaspoon flavoring per ¼ cup salt.

Mussels with Spring Onions, Sorrel, Cider, and Cream

- 4 pounds live mussels
- 4 slices bacon, diced
- 4 spring onions, chopped
- 2 cups sorrel leaves, julienned (optional)
- 3 cloves garlic, thinly sliced
- 4 thyme sprigs, lightly chopped
- 1 teaspoon kosher salt
- 2 cups hard cider
- 1 cup heavy cream
- Flat-leaf parsley, chopped, for garnish
- Crusty bread, for serving

Blue mussels grow down on the tide line in coastal Alaska, and they're best harvested in the winter and spring when phytoplankton activity is lowest. These sweet shellfish make a delightful spring meal with crusty bread for mopping up all the tasty sauce. If possible, these beauties are best enjoyed by the seaside.

Warning: Though we love heading out with a bucket and boots to harvest our own at low tide, we don't mess around with red tide, also known as paralytic shellfish poisoning (PSP), which can be deadly if ingested. If you're unsure about the safety of your locally harvested seafood, buy shellfish from a local grower who tests for the toxins so you can enjoy your mussels without fear.

Makes about 4 servings

Rinse, scrub, and debeard the mussels under cold water. If any are slightly open, tap them. If they close, they are still alive and ready to cook; if they remain open, they are dead—discard them.

In a large Dutch oven or stockpot over medium-high heat, cook the bacon, stirring often, until it turns brown and crisp, about 5 minutes. Drain on paper towels, leaving the bacon grease in the pot.

Add the spring onions, sorrel, garlic, thyme, and salt to the pot and stir for 1 minute. Add the cider, bring to a boil, then reduce the heat to a simmer and cook until the cider is reduced by half, about 10 to 15 minutes. Increase the heat to medium-high, add the mussels, cover the pot, and cook until all the mussels open, 5 to 8 minutes. Stir in the cream and sprinkle in the reserved bacon and the parsley. Serve with crusty bread on the side.

Rhubarb-Mint Gin & Tonic

FOR THE SYRUP:
2 cups chopped rhubarb
½ cup sugar
½ cup water

FOR THE COCKTAIL:
Ice cubes
1½ ounces gin
1 ounce rhubarb syrup
1 wedge lime
3 fresh mint leaves
3 ounces tonic water

A quick trip to your rhubarb patch will reward you with this refreshing cocktail. The multipurpose rhubarb syrup can be poured over pancakes or ice cream or stored in the refrigerator until five o'clock strikes. The rest is simple. For a nonalcoholic elixir, skip the gin.

Makes 1 serving

To make the rhubarb syrup, in a medium saucepan over medium-high heat, bring the rhubarb, sugar, and water to a boil. Lower the heat to medium-low and simmer until the rhubarb is soft, 20 to 30 minutes. Remove from the heat and strain through a fine-mesh sieve, pressing the rhubarb pulp to get as much liquid out as possible. Pour the syrup into a glass jar or bottle and store in the refrigerator for up to 2 weeks.

To make the cocktail, put ice cubes in a glass and add the gin and rhubarb syrup. Squeeze a wedge of lime over the glass, then drop it in. Add the mint leaves. Top with the tonic water, stir gently, and serve.

STORIES FROM ALASKAN WOMEN ON THRIVING IN SPRING

"Put your skis away before the snow is gone or you will never get all your boat work done. Mail your clean clothes and fresh pillow to your remote fishing location, one week before you think you should, so it's there at the post office when you arrive. Get your studded tires off your car, take it to the car wash, and detail the inside with wet wipes. Drive with the window open! Always have a wool hat and a puffy jacket in your car for chilly evening beach parties."

—CATIE BURSCH, HOMER, ALASKA (DENA'INA LAND)

"I've found that I need to pace myself and truly embrace the fact that spring is a time of transition. It's hard not to dive in headfirst and fill up my schedule from dawn to dusk as we all reemerge from our hibernation, eager to reconnect with each other, reunite with our favorite trails, and catch up on yard projects that we've neglected all winter. If I dive into spring too fast, I find myself overwhelmed before summer has even begun. I think it's important that we all give ourselves permission to gradually ease in and prepare for all the beautiful, delicious, and thrilling things that summer has to offer in Alaska."

—ELIZABETH HERENDEEN, JUNEAU, ALASKA (TLINGIT LAND)

Forage Spruce Tips

Head out into the springtime spruce trees to gather an aromatic Alaskan delicacy, spruce tips. With their bright-green color and citrusy, herbal flavor, these little tree buds are easy to spot and a delicious complement to both sweet and savory dishes, as well as drinks.

Spruce trees can be identified by their sharp and pointy branches, and you'll know the tips are ready to harvest the moment they begin to pop through the brown papery skin. The perfect time for picking is when the tips have mostly emerged but are still small. To harvest, simply pluck the small green tips from the ends of the spruce branches with your fingers. The tips' flavor changes to bitter and the texture toughens as they mature. If you think you've missed the optimum harvesting window, hike up to higher elevation, where you'll likely find fresher, younger growth.

Spruce tips make a wonderful flavor for syrup, salt seasoning, shortbread cookies, and cocktails; some Alaskan brewers even use it in their beer recipes. They can also be harvested and frozen for safekeeping into the summer, fall, and winter. It's best to chop them while still frozen, and if you notice their color in the freezer starting to dull or yellow, they've grown stale and can be used for garden mulch. With your harvest, try making Spruce-Tip Ice Cream (page 67) or your own spruce tip–infused sea salt (see Make Your Own Sea Salt, page 57) to sprinkle on the first salmon of the season.

Spruce-Tip Ice Cream

2 cups heavy cream
1¼ cups whole milk
⅔ cup sugar
⅛ teaspoon fine sea salt
5 egg yolks
½ cup spruce tips

Courtesy of Wild Scoops Handcrafted Alaskan Ice Cream

Late spring is Alaskan spruce-tip season. The ends of spruce tree boughs are covered with vibrant green and supple tips, the new year's growth. If you pick the tips right around the time they are shedding their papery cap, the flavor is citrusy-floral, and divine. Spruce-tip beer is popular in Alaska, as are homemade syrups and salts. Spruce-tip ice cream is another special treat. It tastes like a walk in the spring forest! See Forage Spruce Tips (page 64) or find a variety of fresh and frozen spruce-tip suppliers online if you're without access in your area.

Makes about 6 cups

In a 4-quart saucepan over medium-high heat, warm the cream, milk, sugar, and salt until the mixture begins to steam, about 5 minutes. Remove the pan from the heat. This is the "hot cream mix."

In a medium bowl, whisk the yolks. Whisking constantly, slowly add about a cup of the hot cream mix into the yolk bowl. Slowly add another cup of the mix while whisking. (This process, known as tempering, gradually warms the eggs with small amounts of hot liquid to keep them from scrambling.)

Pour the yolk-cream mixture back into the saucepan with the rest of the mix. Over medium-low heat, gently cook until the mixture is thick enough to coat the back of a spoon (about 170 degrees F on a kitchen thermometer).

Cool the mixture by setting the pan inside a larger bowl or pot filled with ice water and stirring occasionally.

After about half an hour, add the spruce tips and stir well. At this point, an immersion blender is handy, but a traditional blender also works well. Blend the mixture until the spruce tips are just green flecks.

Finish chilling the mixture in the refrigerator for 12 to 24 hours to let the spruce flavors steep and bloom.

Strain the ice cream base into a large bowl using cheesecloth or a fine-mesh strainer (discard the spruce tips). Pour the mixture into an ice cream machine and churn according to the manufacturer's instructions. While it's churning, chill a shallow plastic container in the freezer. Serve directly from the machine for soft serve or, to serve later, transfer the ice cream to the chilled container, top with parchment paper, and store in the freezer.

Summer

Gold flecks on the evening water sparkle like the scales of a wild salmon, the sunset lingering into the early morning. Summer brings the sun high in the sky, bright and beaming, shaking us awake from our boat bunks with the feeling that we've already slept through too much of the useful daylight. The indoors have become uncomfortable and the outdoors home to all creatures. Find us on the water with fish scales in our hair and the ocean swell in our eyes. We haven't been to land in days, town in weeks, home in months, and we're thinking more like fish everyday as salmon oil tunes up our bodies and brains and softens our skin and hair. Gulls, seals, puffins, and orcas remind us of our place in the natural cycle, all of us creatures on the hunt for our next meal. The wind and tide are a constant force, tugging and pushing, offering us something to lean into and flow over, something to remind us of the direction we're headed or being blown.

Our fishing boat is our floating home, with bins under benches full of dry and canned food. We are self-sufficient at sea; we make do with what we have on board or trade with friends on other boats. We pull up our pot full of sweet, plump shrimp or drop a line and hope for a halibut or cod. When we anchor up, we paddle into shore to pick beach greens full of vitamin C, wild parsley, or urchins at low tide.

Our friends on land are in the mountains, sitting among berry bushes with purple fingers, mosquito bites, and scratched-up legs. Their hands are full of wildflower bouquets, their legs strong from long days on land. Their gardens have taken off and kitchen counters overflow with ripe tomatoes and tender greens. Weekends are spent chest deep in the river or out in a skiff catching salmon, biking and hiking through fields of fireweed, and tasting the first sweet wild strawberries, salmonberries, and blueberries of summer. By the summer solstice, most of Alaska's fisheries have begun, salmon summer is in full force, and communities are nourished with the wild powers of the sea.

The season is full, ripe, and charged with hard work and wild food. Go outside and exist alongside the flowers, berries, and fish; foster your relationship with the land and sea. Nourish your active body, wild soul, and celebrate the rich abundance around you.

Pick Wild Berries

COMMON BERRIES TO LOOK FOR IN ALASKA:

- blueberries
- raspberries
- cloudberries
- lingonberries (or low-bush cranberries)
- highbush cranberries
- salmonberries
- crowberries

Berry picking is a serious enterprise for many Alaskans in the late summer, heading out to their favorite berry patches to pick until their fingers turn purple with wild berry juices. Some folks keep their patches a secret, and some invite their friends and family to share their berry hot spots. Thanks to ongoing stewardship of the land, there are enough berries to go around even without precise coordinates or passed-down family tradition.

Berries are prized in Alaska because they're delicious fresh, frozen, dried, preserved, baked with, and used in a traditional Native Alaskan ice cream called *akutaq*, a Yup'ik word meaning "mix them together," in this case, seal oil and berries. They're also full of powerful antioxidants, which help protect cells from aging and disease. According to a 2006 University of Alaska study, wild-picked lingonberries have nearly eight and a half times the amount of antioxidants as blueberries cultivated in the Lower 48.

We love berry picking because it's a variation on regular hiking that includes built-in snack breaks. Finding a comfy blueberry bush to sit in or lying in the warm berry-laden tundra and filling a bucket with sweet wild food is as heavenly as it sounds, and one of our favorite summer pastimes. We bring a few ziplock bags, small buckets, or empty yogurt containers to collect berries and a backpack to store our haul for hands-free hiking in case we take a tumble. We always make sure to look out for bears, which also love the berry patch, and make conversation or sing as we go, so as not to surprise them. There are also poisonous berries in Alaska, most of which are white in color, including the deadly baneberry, so bring an identification book or guide with you to know which types to avoid. *Discovering Wild Plants: Alaska, Western Canada, the Northwest* by Janice Schofield is a favorite of ours.

Super Berry Muffins

- 1 cup all-purpose, whole wheat, or oat flour, plus more as needed
- ½ cup old-fashioned rolled oats
- 3 teaspoons baking powder
- ½ teaspoon baking soda
- ½ teaspoon ground cinnamon
- ¼ teaspoon kosher salt
- 1 large egg
- 1 cup plain Greek yogurt
- ⅔ cup honey
- ¼ cup unsweetened almond milk
- 2 tablespoons vegetable oil
- 2 tablespoons dark brown sugar, plus more for topping
- 2 teaspoons vanilla extract
- 1 cup berries, fresh or frozen

Packable, snackable, hearty and made with healthy ingredients that will keep your gears turning all day, these just might be the perfect muffins. Use any berries from your summer harvest—add them in straight from the bush or from the stockpile growing in your freezer. Enjoy these muffins fresh out of the oven slathered with butter and honey, or pack them for the perfect trail snack.

Makes 12 muffins

Preheat the oven to 350 degrees F and grease a muffin pan or use paper muffin liners.

In a medium bowl, combine the flour, oats, baking powder, baking soda, cinnamon, and salt.

In a large bowl, whisk together the egg, yogurt, honey, almond milk, vegetable oil, brown sugar, and vanilla.

Add the dry ingredients to the wet ingredients, mixing gently until just combined. Toss the berries in a tablespoon of flour to prevent them from bleeding or sinking to the bottom of the muffins and fold them gently into the batter.

Divide the batter evenly among the muffin cups, filling almost to the top. Sprinkle with oats and sugar, if desired.

Bake until the tops of the muffins are firm to the touch and a skewer inserted into the center comes out clean, 20 to 22 minutes. Allow the muffins to cool in the pan for 5 minutes, then transfer them to a wire rack to cool completely, or enjoy them warm from the oven. Store muffins in an airtight container at room temperature for up to 5 days.

Cast-Iron Baked Eggs

- 3 tablespoons unsalted butter
- 3 cups finely sliced sweet onion or shallot
- Kosher salt and freshly ground black pepper
- 1 cup torn or chopped greens, such as spinach or kale
- ½ cup cherry tomatoes, sliced in half
- 6 to 8 eggs
- 1 cup grated white cheddar, mozzarella, or Parmesan cheese
- 2 green onions, both white and green parts, finely chopped, for topping
- Your favorite hot sauce, for topping
- Buttered toast, for serving

This easy one-pan dish, our favorite way to make eggs for a group, takes just a few minutes cooking on the stovetop and a few more in the oven. Pair with a fresh baguette or buttery toast and make this simple egg bake your own with the ingredients you have on hand. We love to sauté up an allium base, add some greens and tomatoes, and top with green onions, cheese, and hot sauce. If you like, serve with a side of bacon, or throw crispy bacon bits right into the bake. And don't forget the buttery toast.

Makes 4 servings

Preheat the oven broiler to high. Melt the butter in a large nonstick oven-proof skillet over medium-high heat. Add the onions, season with salt and pepper, and cook, stirring occasionally, until the onions are soft and tender, about 12 minutes. Add the greens and tomatoes and cook for another 2 minutes.

With a spoon or spatula, make egg-size wells in the vegetables and crack an egg into each; season with salt and pepper and sprinkle with the cheese.

Transfer the skillet to the broiler and cook until the eggs are still soft and runny in the center but the whites are cooked through, 1 to 2 minutes. Be careful not to overcook the eggs. Prepare buttered toast while the eggs are in the broiler. Divide the eggs among four plates and serve over or alongside toast with a sprinkle of chopped green onions and hot sauce.

Celebrate the First Fish

Sustenance for many people of the Northwest Coast has depended on the return of migrating salmon each summer. Alaska's Native inhabitants have lived by a complex system of balance and reciprocity with the environment for thousands of years, and as relative newcomers to this land, it is our responsibility and honor to learn from its original caretakers and treat the land's gifts with respect. As a fishing family, honoring the first fish that swims into our net each summer is an important act of reverence for the creatures that provide our livelihood and healthy food for our community. The return of the summer salmon is also a celebration, a time of joy and renewal that reminds us that we are a part of the rhythmic cycles of nature and the interdependence of all beings. It is a time of gratitude—for making it through another winter and for the return of these life-giving fish.

Paying respect to your first catch of the season, whether you depend on salmon for sustenance or simply enjoy eating them, is a tradition that can be honored by all. Dedicating energy in the form of a small ceremony, a prayer, poem, song, or simple words of thanks that feel true to your relationship with salmon, along with the careful preparation of your catch, is a meaningful way to give thanks to the Swimmers who provide us with sustenance and strength. After gathering with friends and family to give thanks, prepare and eat your first fish and return her bones and fins to the water so that her friends will know that she has been treated with respect. Maybe they too will swim into your net and bring health, strength, and a bountiful fishing season.

Make Salmon Caviar

SUPPLIES LIST

- galvanized mesh or screen (about ¼ inch), or a tennis racket
- a few large bowls
- large strainer
- 1-gallon ziplock bag
- salmon roe
- kosher salt
- cold water

Salmon caviar is brined roe, also enjoyed as *ikura* in Japan and *lososevaya ikra* in Russia. These ruby-red pearls burst against the palate in a salty-sweet tang, nourishing your body with omega-3 fatty acids that stave off heart disease, diabetes, depression, and inflammation. In Alaska, bears take advantage of this powerful nutrition, feeding exclusively on a luxurious diet of roe and brains when salmon are spawning.

In Japan and Russia, chum (keta) salmon roe is prized for caviar because its eggs are bigger than those of other species; however, caviar can be made at home from any wild salmon roe. Over half of the world's salmon roe comes from North American waters, a large percentage from Alaska and the Pacific Northwest. Many subsistence and recreational fishermen cure the roe from salmon they catch and enjoy it at home, and you can too. It's an easy process; the main obstacle for most people is obtaining fresh salmon eggs. During the salmon run in June through August, fresh eggs can be found in abundance if you catch your own fish or have the right connections with a fisherman or reputable fish buyer.

Salmon roe should be handled with care. Fresh from the salmon, the eggs will be covered in skeins, a membrane holding the eggs together. Keep the eggs cold at all times but do not freeze them, which will kill their sensuous pop and silky texture.

First, remove the eggs from the skein: Set a mesh, screen, or tennis racket over a large bowl. Spread each skein membrane side up and work the skein gently back and forth over the mesh until the eggs individually release and fall through the screen.

Next, make a brine: Fill another large bowl with cold water and dissolve enough salt in it to make a saturated saline solution with no undissolved excess salt in the bottom of the bowl.

Add the separated eggs to the cold brine and stir gently. Let the eggs brine for 10 minutes.

Test for saltiness: Take a spoonful of eggs and place in a strainer. Rinse them in fresh water and taste. If they're not salty enough, leave in the brine for another 5 minutes and then taste again. When the eggs are to your liking, pour them into the strainer and rinse them with cold water, stirring gently with your fingers to wash off the salt.

Place the drained strainer of eggs back over a large bowl and fill a gallon ziplock bag with cold water. Place the bag on top of the caviar as a gentle compress and refrigerate overnight. In the morning, transfer the roe to a glass jar or other sealable container. Store in the refrigerator for up to a week. Enjoy the salmon caviar on crackers, sushi, rice bowls, baked potatoes, scrambled eggs, blinis, and more. Homemade caviar is a food to be enjoyed "in the moment" rather than preserved, so eat it on everything until it's gone!

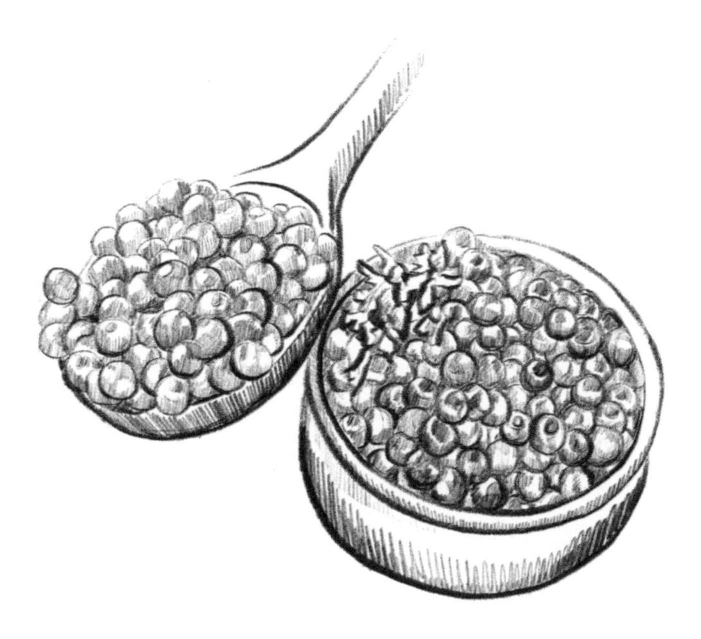

Fancy Toast with Homemade Ricotta and Salmon Caviar

TOOLS NEEDED

Colander, cheesecloth, heavy-bottomed stockpot with lid, wooden spoon, and a bowl

FOR THE RICOTTA:

8 cups whole milk (not ultra-pasteurized)
½ teaspoon salt, plus more for seasoning
1 large lemon, first zested, then juiced
1 tablespoon fresh thyme leaves
Freshly ground black pepper

FOR THE TOAST:

1 loaf rustic sourdough or rye, thickly sliced
1 to 2 cups arugula or mixed baby greens
Avocado, sliced
Sea salt
1 small jar (about 2 ounces) of salmon caviar

This delicious lunch or appetizer is made special with simple homemade ricotta, topped with a summer delicacy from the sea—salmon roe, also known as *ikura* or caviar. We love curing our own salmon roe in season (see Make Salmon Caviar, page 80), but jarred varieties are available in specialty grocery stores and fish markets. Ricotta is easy to make at home, but you can skip this step and save some time by picking up a quality store-bought variety. Start with a good loaf of rustic bread and try other variations like a fancy roast with ricotta, roasted asparagus, and grilled lemon; avocado and sea salt; or a tomato medley salad with balsamic glaze.

Makes 4 servings

To make the ricotta, line a colander with dampened cheesecloth that has been folded over at least three times. Place the colander over a large bowl. In a large heavy-bottomed pot over medium heat, heat the milk. (Note: use a pot made of nonreactive metal, such as stainless steel or enameled cookware. Avoid aluminum, copper, and cast iron, which can negatively affect the flavor.) When the milk is warm, add the salt and stir occasionally with a wooden spoon, making sure the milk does not scorch on the bottom of the pot.

Continue to slowly heat the milk until it registers 185 degrees F on a thermometer, about 20 minutes. Turn the heat to low and add the lemon juice. Using a wooden spoon, gently agitate the milk until you see small curds begin to form, 2 to 3 minutes. It will look like it is separating . . . because it is! The curds are separating from the whey.

Remove from the heat. Cover the pot with a lid and let it sit about 25 minutes. ⟶

Gently ladle the curds into the cheesecloth-lined colander placed over a bowl. The firmness of the cheese will depend on how long you leave the ricotta to drain. For a creamier ricotta, let it sit for just 3 to 5 minutes. Gently twist the cheesecloth to squeeze out that last bit of excess liquid. Transfer the ricotta to a bowl and refrigerate for 20 minutes to cool and set up.

Fold in the reserved lemon zest and thyme and season to taste with salt and pepper.

Toast a few thick slices of crusty bread, slather each with a generous dollop of fresh ricotta and garnish with the fresh greens, avocado, a spoonful of caviar, and a sprinkle of sea salt.

STORIES FROM ALASKAN WOMEN ON TREASURED SUMMER FOOD TRADITIONS

"Once the salmon start to come in greater numbers, we get a call on the VHF radio saying that it's 'time to smoke fish.' We all gear up, kids in tow, to split, brine, and hang the fish. Grandma Gassy will start her smokehouse and start the ten-day process of lighting the smokehouse and hanging them out on the nicer days to speed up the drying and smoking process. When the smoked fish is done, we savor it with fresh bread and a cup of tea."

—CARLEEN HOBLET, FALSE PASS, ALASKA (UNANGAX̂ LAND)

"Piling into a skiff with friends to go out to a certain point in the bay where the sea asparagus grows thick. Lingering June sunshine warm on our backs in the long Alaska evening as we clip, nibbling on fresh salty bits as we go. Wind in our faces as we motor home, bags and baskets full of our harvest. Most will be frozen or canned for later, but the first meal is the simplest and best: sautéed fresh with bacon. It's so good, my daughter requests it for her birthday meal."

—BETH ENDER, THORNE BAY, ALASKA (HAIDA LAND)

Harvest Edible Seaweed

COMMON EDIBLE SEAWEEDS IN ALASKA:

- *Alaria marginata* (winged kelp)
- *Undaria pinnatifida* (wakame)
- *Fucus gardneri* (rockweed)
- *Utricularia vulgaris* (popweed)
- *Laminaria* (kelp, kombu)
- *Nereocystis luetkeana* (bull kelp, bullwhip kelp)
- *Porphyra abbottiae* (black seaweed, nori, laver)
- *Palmaria mollis* (ribbon seaweed, dulse)
- *Ulva fenestrata* (sea lettuce)
- *Salicornia virginica* (beach asparagus)

Sample the ocean's garden. There are edible seaweeds of various shapes and sizes occupying a wide array of ecological zones, from high tide down through subtidal zones. Seaweeds not only provide important nearshore ecosystems for invertebrates and fish, but contribute important organics to the ecosystem and are nutritious and delicious for human consumption.

In Alaska, seaweeds have been an important traditional food source for the Haida, Tlingit, Tsimshian, Eyak, and Alutiiq people, and many varieties continue to provide nourishment for Northwest tribes. Black seaweed and ribbon seaweed are important food and trade items. In the Bristol Bay region, rockweed laden with herring eggs is a treasured spring food. West Coast Native people used bull kelp to make rope from the long slender portion of the stipe for marine-related tasks such as anchoring something offshore. The hollow bulb portion of bullwhip kelp was used to store foods, such as oil from the eulachon, a small herring-like fish.

Seaweeds have various minerals, vitamins, carbohydrates, and sometimes protein. Species vary in their vitamin and mineral content, but most are nutritious.

Seaweeds are usually picked in the spring and summer, when abundant light and nutrients provide for rapid new growth. In the spring, the early morning light coincides with good low tides, making picking easier. In the summer, the midnight sun makes anything possible.

Locate a beach accessible by boat or hiking, and assess the water quality and surroundings, being cautious of industrial sites, outfalls, or other contaminants. Try to arrive at the beach at least an hour before low tide to give yourself time to settle in and scout the beach for seaweed. Assess routes to the water's edge and move slowly over slippery rocks.

SUPPLIES LIST

- boots or waders
- rain gear and warm clothes
- survival gear (water, signals, personal flotation devices, phone, radio)
- small pair of scissors or paring knife
- clean bags to hold seaweed (an old pillowcase or onion or mesh bags work well)
- backpack to hold your supplies (for hands-free climbing on slippery rocks)
- large clean tote for transporting seaweed (once you're back in your truck or boat)

If you plan to harvest more than one seaweed, carry several bags and place each type in separate containers. When you're collecting, selectively cut or "thin" seaweeds rather than taking all the growth in one area, leaving the lower portion of fronds and holdfasts on the rocks to preserve important habitat for small animals. Rinse your harvest in the ocean to help remove any small-shelled animals or scum that may have settled on the seaweed from falling tides.

Seaweeds can be enjoyed fresh, cooked, pickled, and dried. If you want to dive deeper into identifying and harvesting Alaska's edible seaweeds, pick up a copy of the Alaska Sea Grant's *Common Edible Seaweeds in the Gulf of Alaska* by Dolly Garza.

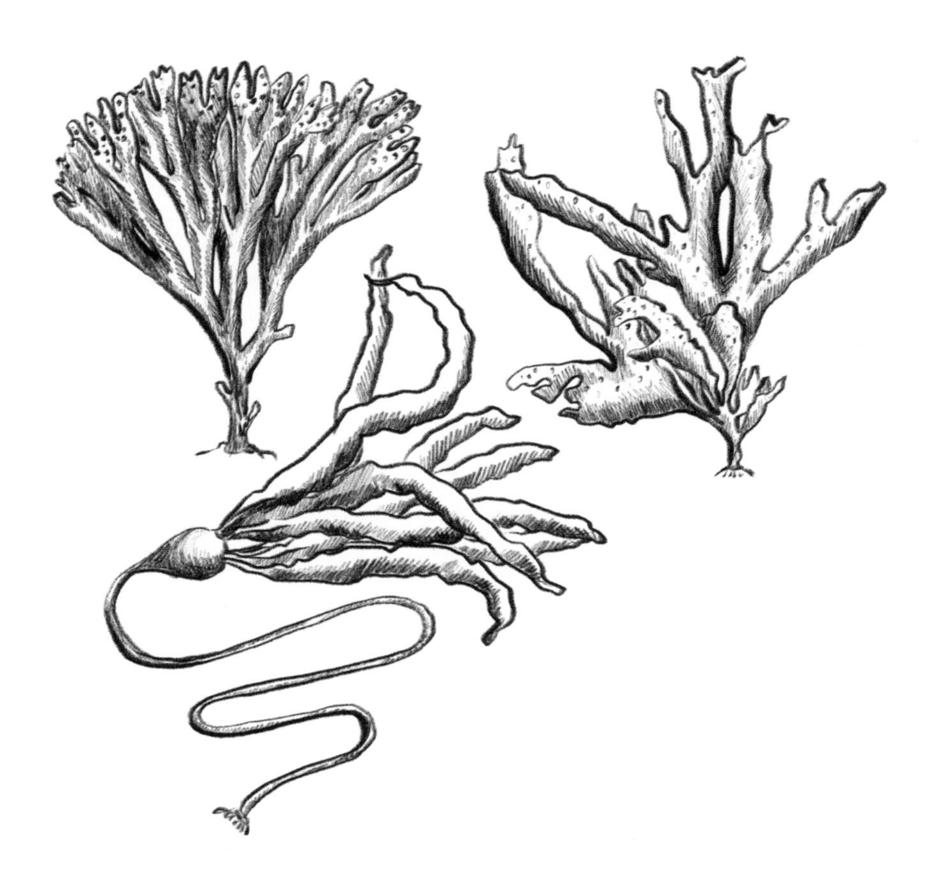

Cured Salmon with Cucumber and Seaweed Salad in Lemony Cream Dressing

FOR THE SALMON CURE:
1 fillet (about 24 ounces) wild salmon, skin removed
½ cup coarse sea salt
½ cup dark brown sugar

FOR THE SALAD:
½ cup extra-virgin olive oil
⅓ cup canola oil
3 tablespoons white wine vinegar
1 large shallot, minced
2 teaspoons dried seaweed flakes (such as furikake), plus more to garnish
Pinch of sea salt
1 large cucumber

FOR THE DRESSING:
2 egg yolks
2 teaspoons dried seaweed flakes
2 teaspoons Dijon mustard
2 teaspoons granulated sugar
2 tablespoons freshly squeezed lemon juice
½ cup canola oil
⅔ cup heavy cream
Sea salt

We love curing salmon overnight in the refrigerator and slicing it into thin lox to enjoy in a scramble, on bagels with cream cheese, or chopped into an imaginative salad. We love the combination of the cured salmon with crunchy, quick-pickled cucumbers and a lemony dressing. It makes for a cooling lunch or appetizer that's easy to prepare in advance and assemble quickly—and beautifully!—for your guests.

Makes 4 servings

To cure the salmon, lay the fish on a tray and sprinkle evenly with the salt and sugar, then turn over to season the other side until the fish is evenly coated all over. If your salmon fillet is large, you may increase the quantities of sea salt and brown sugar in a 1-to-1 ratio to ensure both sides of the fillet are covered. Wrap the whole tray tightly with plastic wrap and refrigerate to cure for 6 hours.

To make the salad, in a small saucepan over medium heat, add the oils, vinegar, shallot, seaweed, and a pinch of salt and bring to a boil. Simmer for 2 minutes, then remove from the heat and allow the mixture to cool.

Meanwhile, peel the cucumber, halve it lengthwise, then scoop out and discard the seeds. Thinly slice the cucumber into half-moon shapes. Lay the cucumber slices in a dish and pour the cooled oil and vinegar mixture over them. Cover with plastic wrap, pressing it down to keep the cucumbers fully submerged. Let stand for at least 1 hour.

To make the dressing, in a small bowl whisk together the egg yolks, seaweed, mustard, sugar, and lemon juice for 1 minute, then gradually whisk in the canola oil, a little at a time, until fully incorporated. To finish, slowly whisk in the cream, then season to taste with salt. Cover and refrigerate until ready to serve. ⟶

Cured Salmon with Cucumber and Seaweed Salad in Lemony Cream Dressing, continued

When the salmon has finished curing, unwrap the fish and rinse off the cure under cold running water, then pat dry with paper towels. Wrap the fish tightly in plastic wrap and refrigerate for 1 hour to firm up.

To serve, cut the cured salmon into thin (1-centimeter) slices and divide among four plates.

Drain off some of the liquid from the cucumber salad. Arrange some of the cucumber salad over the salmon and spoon on the cream dressing. Finish each plate with a sprinkle of seaweed flakes.

STORIES FROM ALASKAN WOMEN ON CELEBRATING THE SUMMER

"June goes by quickly! We enjoy the beautiful days, and the rainy days as well. The salmonberry bushes need both. Our first couple bowls of berries are usually eaten right up with a box of milk and sugar. The next batches are used to make *akutaq*, a recipe I brought to my family from my Yup'ik roots. We also put some away for the winter, make jam and jelly and pies. In mid-to-late July we wait for a nice day and pack up whoever wants to go for a skiff ride to pick wild strawberries. We barbecue on the beach and the kids play in the ocean. Everyone in the family puts their strawberries together so we can make jam."

—CARLEEN HOBLET, FALSE PASS, ALASKA (UNANGAX̂ LAND)

"We are always at our fish camp for the summer, fishing our sites and putting up salmon. I have a birthday in the middle of the summer (and was actually born at fish camp) and we always have a huge get-together! My mom makes several dozen cupcakes and over two hundred of her homemade ice cream sandwiches, which the whole beach raves about. My whole family are also pilots, and we have many fun adventures flying over to the cape to go beachcombing or flying out and landing on the tundra and picking tons of berries."

—LOGAN BALL, DILLINGHAM, ALASKA (YUP'IK LAND)

"Homemade ice cream and freshly picked berries. Sitting on the front steps after supper to watch the sun set and the boats come in from fishing. Swimming in the ocean until our bodies tingle. Driftwood campfires on the beach. Wildflower bouquets on the table."

—BETH ENDER, THORNE BAY, ALASKA (HAIDA LAND)

Make Fish Jerky

- ½ cup soy sauce
- 2 tablespoons maple or birch syrup
- 1 tablespoon freshly squeezed lemon juice
- 1 teaspoon liquid smoke
- 2 teaspoons freshly ground black pepper
- 1 salmon fillet (about 24 ounces), fresh or thawed

In the season of summer abundance, we enjoy smoking fish and making homemade fish jerky in our dehydrator. A useful tool, a dehydrator can be set up on your kitchen counter or out of the way in your garage to preserve your harvest, be it meat, fish, garden vegetables, mushrooms, other foraged plants, or wild berries.

Fish jerky makes a great anytime protein-packed snack to bring camping, to work, or to slip into your kid's backpack. It's easy to make with any fish, though we love salmon jerky for its perfectly chewy texture and candylike flavor. Once you've tried our basic marinade, play around with your own. Try garlic, chili powder, teriyaki sauce, or your favorite marinade. The jerky world is your oyster.

Makes 3 to 4 cups, depending on the size of the salmon fillet

In a small bowl, combine the soy sauce, syrup, lemon juice, liquid smoke, and pepper.

Strip the salmon fillet lengthwise in ½-inch strips. We like to leave the skin on the strips because it helps hold the jerky pieces together once dried, but if you prefer a skinless snack, remove the skin before stripping. Leave the strips long or cut them into 3- to 4-inch-long pieces, depending on the length of your fillet. Place the salmon pieces in a 1-gallon ziplock bag with the marinade. Seal the bag and shake gently to evenly coat the salmon pieces. Refrigerate for 3 to 4 hours.

Drain the salmon in a colander and pat dry with paper towels. Lay the strips on dehydrator trays, making sure the pieces are not touching. Place the trays in the dehydrator set at 145 degrees F for 3 to 4 hours. Salmon jerky is done when the pieces are dry and chewy, but not crunchy.

Tinned Octopus, Avocado, and Tomato Salad with Lime-Cilantro Dressing

FOR THE DRESSING:

⅔ cup extra-virgin olive oil
1 large lime, first zested, then juiced
2 tablespoons chopped cilantro
1 tablespoon Dijon mustard
Kosher salt and freshly ground black pepper

FOR THE SALAD:

2 (6-ounce) cans smoked octopus, drained and chopped to the desired size
2 ripe avocados, peeled, pitted, and sliced
20 cherry or baby plum tomatoes, halved
4 packed cups arugula leaves
Pinch of salt

Octopus has been a subsistence food in Alaska for thousands of years. We grew up walking the beach at low tide, searching for octopus under big rocks, and sometimes we were lucky enough to harvest one. More recently we've enjoyed sampling tinned octopus and work with Wildfish Cannery, an artisanal cannery in Klawock, Alaska, to source smoked Bering Sea octopus for our shops. Walk the aisle of any specialty grocery or fish market and you might find tinned octopus, which is usually preserved in olive oil, precooked, and ready to add to any meal. Make this fresh and zesty salad in a flash.

Makes 2 to 4 servings

To make the dressing, in a medium bowl, whisk together the oil, lime zest and juice, cilantro, and mustard (or add the ingredients to a jar and shake with the lid tightly closed), and season to taste with salt and pepper.

To make the salad, in a large serving bowl, combine the octopus, avocado, and tomatoes. Add a few spoonfuls of dressing and toss gently, then add the arugula and salt. Share the salad equally between two to four plates and finish with another drizzle of dressing.

Roasted Beets and Carrots with Anchovy-Herb Butter

FOR THE HERB BUTTER:
½ cup (1 stick) unsalted butter, at room temperature
½ cup finely chopped fresh parsley, leaves and tender stems only
¼ cup finely chopped fresh basil
¼ cup very finely chopped fresh chives
4 anchovy fillets, very finely chopped
1 clove garlic, finely grated
2 tablespoons white wine vinegar
Kosher salt and freshly ground black pepper

FOR THE VEGETABLES:
1 bunch small, tender carrots with green, leafy tops
2 medium beets
3 tablespoons extra-virgin olive oil
1 lemon, halved
Flaky sea salt and freshly ground black pepper

We love to roast the bright carrots and beets growing in our garden. Though the growing season in the North is short, the midnight sun fosters sun-drenched flavors and Alaska-size vegetables. Adding an anchovy herb butter to your normal sheet pan of roasted veggies brings out a rainbow of earthy flavors. The herb butter can be made up to two weeks ahead, covered tightly, and refrigerated. Bring the butter to room temperature before using.

Makes 4 servings

To make the herb butter, in a medium bowl, combine the butter, herbs, anchovies, garlic, and vinegar. Smash with a fork until well blended or place in a food processor and blend until well combined. Season to taste with salt and pepper.

To prepare the vegetables, preheat the oven to 425 degrees F. Scrub the carrots and halve them lengthwise. Wash and chop the carrot tops. Trim and scrub the beets and slice them into ¼-inch slivers. On a rimmed baking sheet, toss together the carrots (making sure to coat the leaves), beets, and oil. Roast until the carrots and beets are tender, 15 to 20 minutes.

To serve, spread the herb butter evenly on a serving plate or in a shallow bowl. Top with the roasted vegetables and squeeze the lemon halves over them. Sprinkle with salt and pepper to taste.

Fried Oyster Toast

1 dozen medium or large oysters, shucked and drained
Peanut or vegetable oil, for frying

FOR THE CAJUN FLOUR:
½ cup all-purpose flour
½ cup masa or fine cornmeal
½ teaspoon paprika
½ teaspoon cayenne
½ teaspoon onion powder
½ teaspoon garlic powder
½ teaspoon ground cumin
½ teaspoon chili powder
½ teaspoon kosher salt
½ teaspoon black pepper
¼ teaspoon dried thyme
¼ teaspoon dried oregano

FOR THE TOAST:
4 pieces thick-cut bread slices (country loaf or Texas toast)
Mayonnaise
Thickly sliced tomatoes
Kosher salt and freshly ground black pepper
Shredded iceberg lettuce
Sliced pickles
Hot sauce or mustard (optional)

When we're salmon fishing in Prince William Sound, we always try to make time for a special trip into the oyster farm tucked away on Perry Island. If they're operating, we call by VHF radio to place an order, and the oyster farmers motor out in their skiff to deliver a sack to our boat. After eating our fill, we sit on deck shucking the large oysters to fry up later using this recipe.

Makes 2 servings (1 dozen fried oysters)

Fill a large, heavy-bottom pot with 4 inches of peanut oil and heat over medium-high heat to 375 degrees F.

To make the Cajun flour, in a small bowl, combine the flour, masa, spices, and herbs.

Dredge the oysters in the flour mixture and carefully add them to the hot oil. The oysters will make a lot of noise at first—keep a safe distance from the pot. When the oysters quiet down, they're finished cooking. Using tongs or a slotted spoon, carefully lift the oysters out of the oil and drain on paper towels.

Toast the bread. Spread mayonnaise on the toast. Arrange the tomatoes on top and season to taste with salt and pepper. Top with the lettuce, pickles, fried oysters, and hot sauce or mustard. Serve open-faced.

Tinned Salmon Niçoise Sandwich

¼ cup mayonnaise
1 anchovy fillet, chopped, or ½ teaspoon anchovy paste
2 small cloves garlic, pressed or minced
2 teaspoons freshly squeezed lemon juice
2 (6-ounce) cans wild smoked salmon
⅓ cup mixed olives, pitted and sliced, such as Kalamata or Castelvetrano
⅓ cup mix of sweet-and-sour pickled peppers in oil or Peppadew peppers, sliced, liquid reserved
1 tablespoon capers, drained
1 small red onion, sliced
½ small cucumber, seeded and cut into ½-inch cubes
1 cup fresh basil leaves, torn
2 tablespoons good-quality extra-virgin olive oil
Kosher salt and freshly ground pepper
1 baguette or 2 large crusty rolls
2 tablespoons whole grain mustard
2 cups baby arugula or mixed greens
1 heirloom or vine-ripened tomato, thickly sliced
1 hard-boiled egg, sliced

This tangy, savory, herby, delightful sandwich comes with a hint of smokiness from the salmon. Packed with pickled and fresh vegetables and finished with a touch of creamy anchovy mayo, it makes for an easy, protein-packed lunch to share around the table or pack for a day outside—no cooking necessary!

Makes 2 servings

In a small bowl, mix the mayonnaise, anchovy, garlic, and lemon juice until well combined. Taste the mixture and adjust with more lemon juice and salt, if necessary. (There are plenty of components in this sandwich that are briny and/or salty, so less is more at this stage.)

Place the salmon in a medium bowl. Using a rubber spatula or large spoon to maintain the integrity of the fish, gently add the olives, peppers, and capers. Adjust the amounts to your personal taste, keeping a balance of salty and sweet. If more sweetness is needed at the end, add a tablespoon of the reserved liquid from the sweet peppers. Fold in the onion, cucumber, basil, and oil and taste again. Season to taste with salt and pepper.

Slice the baguette in half and spread each side with a thick layer of the mayonnaise, then the mustard. Place the greens on the bottom half of the bread and top with slices of tomato. Spoon on the salmon mixture, top with the egg and the second slice of bread, and enjoy!

Cook Fish over a Fire

Most of our favorite summer meals are cooked on the beach over a driftwood fire with an ocean view. When we have a day off during the fishing season, we save a fresh salmon to enjoy together on land, where we can cook outside and look back at the sun glistening on the water and the boats anchored offshore. The salty sea breeze and the smell of salmon on the fire is one of our absolute favorite things.

Whether you live near the shore where driftwood abounds, or your backyard fire pit is your closest wilderness, cooking a fish outside is a simple and especially flavorful way to savor the season.

Start by building a driftwood fire, or use any untreated wood like alder, maple, or cedar. Let the fire burn into a hot bed of coals. If you have a grill grate with legs, position it over the coals, otherwise walk down the beach to find a rock that is large, thin, and flat to prop above the coals as a grill surface. Let the stone heat up while you prepare the fish for cooking. Fillet the salmon and place the portions skin side down on the grate or stone. Drizzle with olive oil, sprinkle sea salt, and squeeze lemon juice over the fish while it cooks. Although cooking time will depend on the heat of the grill and the thickness of the fish, the fish is done when the fillet begins to flake when tested with a fork and is slightly translucent at its thickest part. Drizzle again with olive oil and some more lemon juice and add any fresh or wild herbs (we like foraging wild petrushki from the shore, which has a strong parsleylike taste). Use a metal spatula to flake fish into serving-size portions. The skin will likely stick to the stone or grate and can be removed separately with a spatula to be enjoyed as an oily, crispy snack, like a chip. Savor the smoky flavor and let the salmon oil soak into your fingers and lips, nourishing your whole body.

Smoky Citrus, Soy, and Herb Cedar-Plank-Grilled Salmon

TOOLS NEEDED

1 untreated cedar grilling plank

FOR THE GLAZE:

¼ cup freshly squeezed orange juice
¼ cup freshly squeezed lemon juice
¼ cup rice wine vinegar
¼ cup maple syrup
2 tablespoons soy sauce
1 teaspoon packed dark brown sugar
1 teaspoon minced fresh ginger
1 teaspoon minced garlic
Pinch of white pepper
6 tablespoons extra-virgin olive oil

FOR THE FISH:

1 wild salmon fillet (about 24 ounces)
1 tablespoon extra-virgin olive oil
Sea salt and freshly ground pepper
1 lemon, thinly sliced
Finely chopped fresh herbs, such as dill, chives, or parsley

Cooking outside with friends is one of the many joys of the fair-weather season. Salmon grilled on a cedar plank is the quintessential taste of an Alaskan summer. Use untreated cedar cooking planks and soak them for at least thirty minutes before grilling. Cook over a medium or medium-low heat so the plank doesn't catch fire. Allow ample cooking time, savor the aromas, and keep a spray bottle with water nearby to extinguish any flare-ups.

Makes 4 to 6 servings

Soak the cedar plank in water for at least 30 minutes.

To make the glaze, in a small saucepan, combine the orange and lemon juice, vinegar, maple syrup, soy sauce, brown sugar, ginger, garlic, and white pepper. Stirring constantly, bring to a boil, then reduce the heat and continue cooking at a low boil until the mixture has thickened and reduced to a syrupy consistency. Remove from the heat and whisk in the oil.

To prepare the salmon, leave the fillet whole or cut it into 4 to 6 portions. Drizzle salmon with olive oil, and sprinkle with sea salt and freshly ground pepper. You do not need to remove the skin; it will be easy to remove once it's cooked.

Preheat a gas grill on medium heat. If you are cooking over an open fire, light the coal and let the flames burn down to a hot, glowing bed of coals. Drain the cedar plank and place the fish, skin side down, on the plank.

Brush each piece of fish generously with the glaze and top with sliced lemons. Place the plank on the grill rack. Cook the fish just until the salmon flakes when tested with a fork and is slightly translucent at its thickest part, 10 to 15 minutes. (Another sign of doneness: when you see the first little spots of white liquid begin to ooze from the flesh of the fish.) Top generously with fresh herbs and serve immediately.

Share Your Harvest with Your Community

Harvesting wild food provides affordable, fresh, and nutritious plants and protein to many Alaskan diets. And for many, the act of going out to hunt, fish, and gather is healthy and meaningful beyond the plate. The wild harvest provides a connection to the land, community, and friends. Whether you go deer or moose hunting in the fall, trapping in the winter, foraging in the spring, or fishing or berry picking in the summer, Alaska's wild resources are abundant and provide a surplus that allows those who can harvest to share with those who can't.

Hunting, fishing, and gathering for others provide intimate community services that are incredibly meaningful for people who have lost the mobility or ability to gather their own wild food. This includes elders, youth, food-insecure community members, sick individuals, busy families, and even friends who are living far from the source and need the nourishment of home.

For Alaska residents, proxy hunting and gathering regulations allow resident hunters to harvest certain fish and game species for elders or residents with a disability. Of course, you can also share your harvest with anyone you like under your own license and bag limit as well. Dropping a few salmon off in an empty freezer or a bucket of sweet wild strawberries on someone's doorstep is a powerful way to care for your community and let someone know they are loved.

During our commercial fishing season, there are opportunities to donate a portion of our catch to local schools, food banks, or senior care centers. We also donate wild fish through Salmon Sisters to the Food Bank of Alaska, which gets distributed to urban and rural communities around the state. The Alaska Food Code allows the donation of food, including wild game meat, seafood, and fish from permitted food establishments, to food banks and other nonprofit organizations. Recreational hunters and fishermen can contact their local food pantry or food bank for procedures for donating their wild harvest. There may be a specific fund in place to help pay for processing costs—as any meat donation must be from USDA-certified processors—and other programs established for distributing wild foods. Your donations will help your local community stay healthy, nourished, and connected to the land.

Miso Salmon and Soba Salad Bowl

FOR THE SALMON:

¼ cup dark aged miso
¼ cup soy sauce
2 tablespoons honey
2 tablespoons rice vinegar
2 (4- to 6-ounce) portions wild Alaska salmon

FOR THE NOODLES:

8 ounces buckwheat soba noodles
1 teaspoon sesame oil

FOR THE VINAIGRETTE:

¼ cup rice wine vinegar
2 tablespoons soy sauce or tamari
1 tablespoon sesame oil
1 tablespoon sugar
1 clove garlic, minced
1 teaspoon grated fresh ginger

FOR THE BOWLS:

1 tablespoon baking soda
2 eggs
1 cup wild mushrooms, such as shiitake, beech, or maitake
Extra-virgin olive oil
Kosher salt
1 bunch spinach, stemmed

This fresh cold soba noodle salad bowl is full of bold umami flavor, fresh greens, and miso-marinated wild sockeye salmon. Protein-packed and alive with superfood nutrients, this gluten-free meal is as delicious as it is gorgeous. We could eat this tasty bowl every day.

Makes 2 servings

To prepare the salmon, in a shallow dish or bowl, mix the miso, soy sauce, honey, and vinegar in a bowl until well blended. Add the salmon portions flesh side down, cover, and marinate in the refrigerator for 2 to 3 hours.

While the fish is marinating, cook the noodles and make the vinaigrette. Bring a large pot of water to a boil and cook the noodles according to the manufacturer's instructions or until just undercooked. Drain and lightly rinse with cool water to stop the cooking process. Add 1 teaspoon of sesame oil and gently massage the noodles to ensure they don't stick together.

To make the vinaigrette, in a pint-size mason jar, add the vinegar, soy sauce, sesame oil, sugar, garlic, and ginger. Seal and give the jar a good shake. Set aside.

To prepare the bowls, fill a medium saucepan with water and add the baking soda. Bring the water to a rolling boil, then reduce to a simmer. Using a slotted spoon, carefully lower each egg into the water and cook for 5 minutes and 30 seconds. Remove the eggs from the pan and immediately place in cold or iced water to stop the cooking.

In a large skillet over medium heat, cook the wild mushrooms in a touch of olive oil until just tender, about 5 minutes; lightly season with salt and remove the mushrooms from the pan. Add the spinach and bok choy to the pan and cook over medium heat until just wilted but still vibrant green, about 30 seconds. ⟶

2 baby bok choy, cut in half lengthwise
1 avocado, peeled, pitted, and sliced
½ small cucumber, seeded and thinly sliced
1 small bunch green onions, both white and green parts, chopped
1 small bunch cilantro, roughly chopped
1 tablespoon white or black sesame seeds

To cook the salmon, preheat the oven broiler on high. Remove the fish from the marinade and pat dry with a paper towel. Place the salmon on a sheet pan and broil until the salmon gently flakes when tested with a fork yet still has a moist and rosy interior, 6 to 10 minutes. (Remember, the fish will continue to cook even after being pulled from the oven. It's best to pull it a touch early and let it "carry-over cook" as it rests to avoid over-cooking the fish. Another trick is to slide a metal skewer or cake tester into the center of the largest part of the fillet, leave it for 15 to 20 seconds and then test against your wrist. If it is cold/cool, it'll need more time. If it is warm to hot, it will be close to done). Set the salmon aside to rest as you begin to assemble the soba bowl.

In a large bowl, toss the cold soba noodles with a touch of the vinaigrette and divide between two serving bowls. Top with the salmon, peeled soft-boiled eggs, mushrooms, spinach, and bok choy. Garnish with the avocado, cucumber, green onions, cilantro, and sesame seeds.

Press Flowers

SUPPLIES LIST

- fresh flowers
- hardcover book
- parchment or printer paper
- stone, brick, or other heavy weight

We are still discovering the flowers we tucked into the old collection of encyclopedias at the top of the bookshelf years ago, collected in the blooming hills and now preserved and flattened into summer memories. Whether you have a project or art piece in mind, or just love flowers, our favorite method is the simplest: press them in a book.

Start by picking flowers in the wild or from your garden as they near full bloom. Pick them in the morning once the dew has evaporated and dry them well to prevent molding before pressing. The best flowers for pressing have flat faces and a single layer of petals, though you can also press larger, thicker, more spherical flowers by separating individual petals from stems or splitting the flower in half.

Gather a sturdy hardcover book, parchment paper to absorb moisture (printer paper, thin cardboard, newspaper, or coffee filters also work), and a heavy weight (a stone, brick, or more heavy books). Fold a piece of paper in half to match the page size of your book and add it to the middle of the book like an extra spread. Try to press flowers of similar thicknesses together and arrange your flowers on the right half of the paper with some space between them, then fold the left side of the paper over the top. Take care to flatten the top of the flower or petal into the desired shape. Carefully close the book and set a weight on top, or pile on more heavy books.

Wait 2 to 4 weeks for the flowers to dry. For thinner flowers, 2 weeks might be just right, while thicker flowers may take closer to 4 weeks. Once dried, the pressed flowers will be very delicate, so handle with care. Pressed flowers can be displayed in glass frames and hung on a wall, laminated into bookmarks, or made into magnets by gluing them onto the back of large flat glass marbles, adding a backing of white paper, a dab of hot glue, and a magnet!

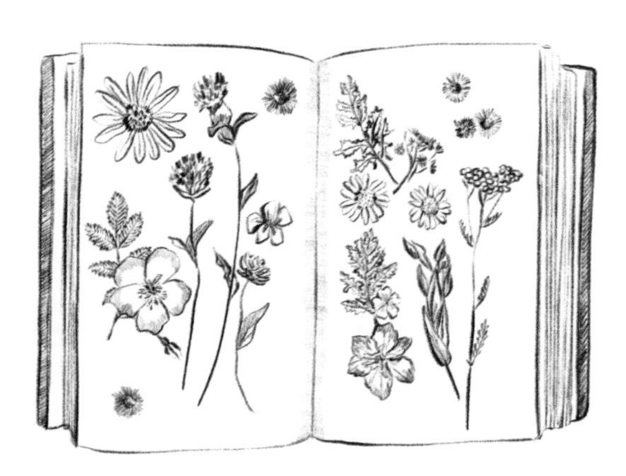

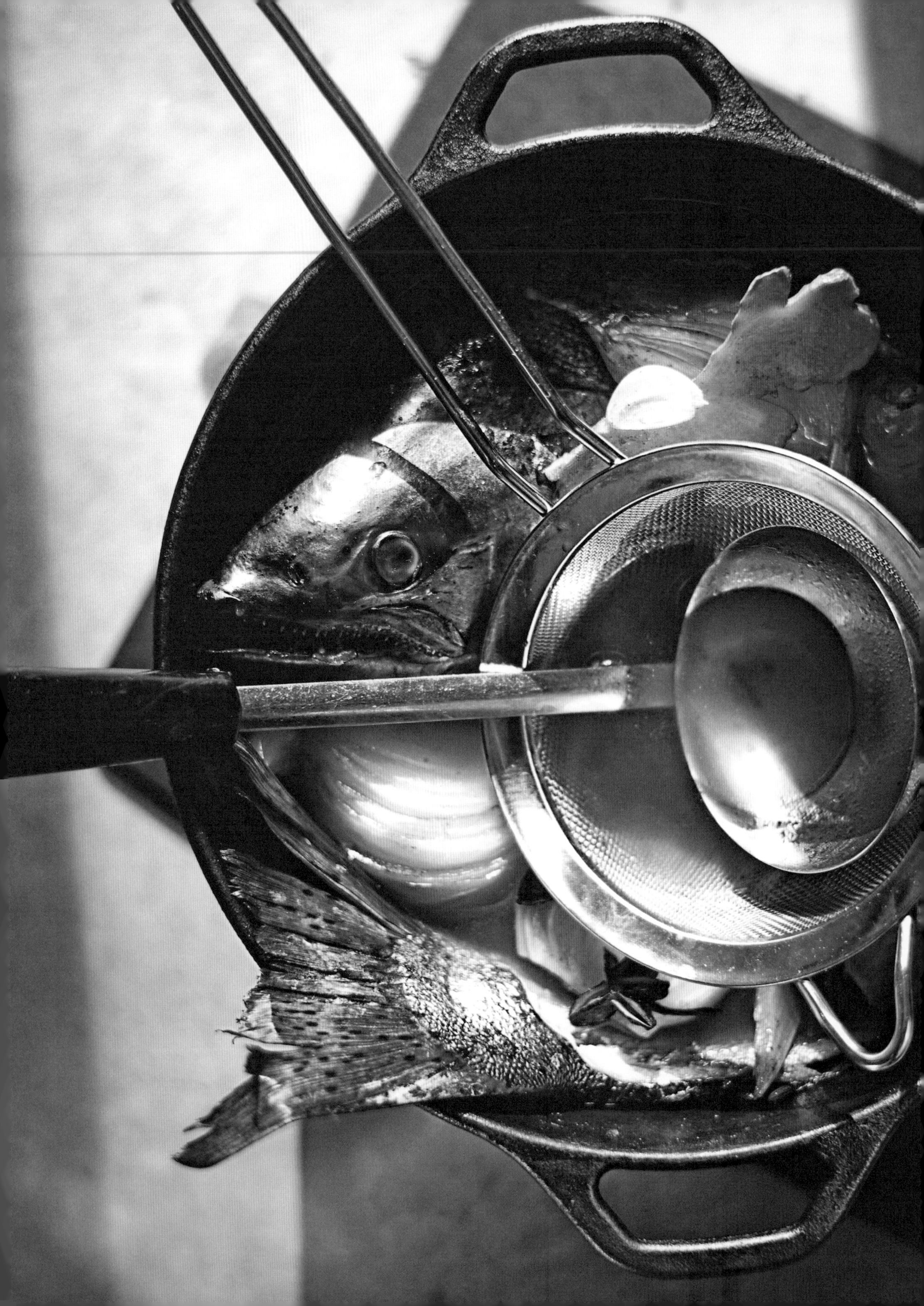

Make Fish Stock

- 2 pounds salmon bones plus the head, rinsed
- 10 cups water
- 2 yellow onions, peeled and cut into large pieces
- 4 cloves garlic, peeled and halved
- 2 medium carrots, washed and cut into 6 pieces each
- 1 stalk celery, cut into pieces
- 2 bay leaves
- 8 sprigs fresh thyme or 2 teaspoons dried thyme
- ¼ cup flat-leaf parsley
- ¼ teaspoon fennel seeds
- 10 black peppercorns, crushed with a mortar and pestle
- 5 whole allspice, crushed
- 2 teaspoons flaky sea salt
- 1 fresh ginger root, peeled and sliced into large pieces
- 3 whole star anise (optional)

Fish stock is useful in so many delicious, savory seafood dishes and incredibly easy to make at home. It's also a smart way to use up a whole fish and use all the nutrient-rich heads and bones, as well as vegetable scraps in your kitchen that might otherwise be wasted. Fish stock keeps well in the freezer for future cooking, so make a big batch when you have the whole fish on hand—your future self will thank you. You can ask for fish carcasses at your local fish counter or freeze bones and heads from fish you catch yourself and make the stock later if you don't have time immediately. Most fish will work for this stock, though we prefer to use wild Alaska salmon. We include the head because it is rich in flavor, but remove the gills and leftover blood and viscera before adding the fish to the stockpot.

Makes about 8 cups stock

Place all the ingredients in a large stockpot. Bring to a full boil over high heat, then reduce to a low, gentle boil. Remove any scum that rises to the top with a spoon and discard. Continue to cook, uncovered, for 50 minutes.

Remove from the heat. Strain the stock through a fine mesh sieve or cheesecloth and discard the solids.

Use the stock immediately, refrigerate for up to 3 days, or freeze for up to 2 months.

Eat Wildflowers

Summer brings an abundance of wildflowers to the Alaskan landscape, and some of the petals, leaves, and stems are edible. Common edible flowers are wild rose (flowers and rose hips), dandelion (flowers and greens), fireweed (flowers and greens), violet (flowers and greens), red clover (flowers and greens), and bluebell (flowers and greens). These blooms are tasty and beautiful atop desserts and salads, or in homemade teas, tinctures, vinegars, jellies, and syrups. (See Fireweed Lemonade, page 124; Sea Salt Fireweed-Honey Pie, page 117; Spring Greens and Flower Salad, page 53; Gather Rose Hips, page 162.)

Sea Salt Fireweed-Honey Pie

FOR THE CRUST:

1¼ cups all-purpose flour
1½ teaspoons sugar
½ teaspoon kosher salt
½ cup (1 stick) cold unsalted butter, cut into ½-inch pieces
½ cup cold water
½ cup ice
2 tablespoons apple cider vinegar

FOR THE FILLING:

¾ cup sugar
½ cup (1 stick) unsalted butter, melted
1 tablespoon white cornmeal
2 teaspoons vanilla extract
½ teaspoon kosher salt
¾ cup fireweed honey
3 eggs
½ cup heavy cream
2 teaspoons white vinegar
1 to 2 teaspoons flaky sea salt, for finishing

This rich, flavorful pie made with honey infused with fireweed, which grows in Southcentral and Southeast Alaska, covering mountainsides and meadows in a blanket of pink in late summer. If you can't find fireweed honey in your area, try any other variety. This recipe is adapted from one of our favorite pies made by Four & Twenty Blackbirds in Brooklyn.

Makes 1 single-crust 9-inch pie

To make the crust, in a large bowl, mix the flour, sugar, and salt. Add the butter pieces and coat with the flour mixture using a spatula. With a pastry cutter, cut the butter into the flour mixture, working quickly, until mostly pea-size pieces of butter remain (a few larger pieces are okay; do not overblend).

In a large measuring cup or small bowl, combine the water, ice, and apple cider vinegar. Sprinkle ice water over the flour mixture 1 tablespoon at a time, mixing the dough with a scraper or spatula until it is fully incorporated and the dough just comes together. It should be moist, but not wet. Shape the dough into a flat disc, wrap in plastic, and refrigerate for at least 1 hour or overnight.

To roll out the pastry, place the disc of chilled dough on a lightly floured surface. Using a floured rolling pin, roll out the dough into a 12-inch circle. Transfer the crust to the pie pan, leaving a 1-inch overhang. Roll and pinch the excess dough under so that it rests on the pan's rim. Crimp the edges.

Transfer the pie pan to the freezer for 1 hour. The dough must be frozen before filling and baking.

To make the filling, preheat the oven to 375 degrees F with a rack in the center position. In a medium bowl, stir together the sugar, melted butter, cornmeal, vanilla, and salt. Stir in the honey and the eggs, one at a time, followed by the cream and vinegar.

Place the frozen pie shell on a rimmed baking sheet and strain the filling through a fine-mesh sieve. Bake for 45 to 50 minutes, rotating the pie when the edges start to set after 30 to 35 minutes. The pie is finished when the edges are set and puffed up high and the center is no longer liquid but jiggles like gelatin and is golden brown on top.

Cool completely on a wire rack, 2 to 3 hours. Sprinkle with flaky sea salt. Serve slightly warm or at room temperature. Store the pie, covered, in the refrigerator for 4 days or at room temperature for 2 days.

STORIES FROM ALASKAN WOMEN ON THRIVING IN SUMMER

"On calm days, the cannery's whistle for 'mug up' carries across the bay, signaling a break for workers, with baked goods and coffee delivered on a golf cart. When the sun is shining, we sit on the grass, ignoring the sticks that our dogs drop patiently next to us while the kids show off their trampoline jumps. If it's raining, we might sit in the hoop house with the hum of fat bumblebees and the scent of tomato plants and sweet peas. On the stormiest days, we watch the waves through the windows from worn recliners that held three nursing babies and so many visiting friends and relatives over the years."

—SARA LOEWEN, UYAK BAY, ALASKA (ALUTIIQ LAND)

"Enjoy the sunshine! Get out in nature and soak in all the beauty that is Alaska."

—HANNAH MCFADDEN, NORTH POLE, ALASKA (TANANA LAND)

"Catch and eat salmon, grow your own salad, and bake rhubarb pies."

—SHELLY LAUKITIS, HOMER, ALASKA (DENA'INA LAND)

"Try a little bit of everything! Make time to truly enjoy being outside. There's no place in the world like Alaska—you have to go out there and experience it all for yourself!"

—JORDYN DAWSON, PALMER, ALASKA (DENA'INA LAND)

"Soak up every day of sunshine, especially here in rainy Southeast Alaska. If the sun is shining, we drop everything that we possibly can and head outdoors. I have never looked back with regret on a day spent outdoors in the sunshine. But, conversely, if anything has changed my perspective on rain, it has been living in Southeast Alaska. You can fish and hike and pick berries in the rain. Rain is soothing, refreshing, and beautiful. Dress appropriately, yes, but don't let it stop you!"

—BETH ENDER, THORNE BAY, ALASKA (HAIDA LAND)

SUMMER SOLSTICE FEAST

MENU

Smoked Salmon Panzanella Salad
page 123

Fireweed (Hard) Lemonade
page 124

Alaska Seafood Boil
page 125

Lemon Olive Oil Cake with Lemony Buttercream Frosting and Blueberries
page 129

Celebrate the first day of summer with a solstice gathering. In the northern hemisphere, the June solstice occurs when the sun travels along its northernmost path in the sky. At its highest point in the sky, it takes longer to rise and set. Host an outdoor celebration on an evening when the weather is fair, taking advantage of the long-lasting sunlight on the longest day of the year.

Set up an outdoor cooking station where you can boil seafood in the open air. Friends and family can pitch in with food prep or sit and enjoy visiting while you cook. Set up a table to gather around and cover it with newspaper. When everything is finished boiling, drain the excess liquid and pour everything out on the table with bowls of melted butter for dipping. It's a fun, messy, delicious affair. Plates and silverware are optional.

If fireweed is blooming, pick some to decorate the table and to add extra blossoms to Fireweed Lemonade—spike it if you like, or leave it simple and refreshing for all ages. Pass around a big bowl of panzanella salad with flaky smoked salmon to bring more savory flavors to the feast. Refresh the palate with fresh vegetables and mop up some of the spiced buttery juices with crusty bread. In the aftermath of the boil, sit back and serve slices of lemony cake covered in freshly picked blueberries and buttercream. Let the evening meander and the good times roll.

Smoked Salmon Panzanella Salad

- 3 cups stale baguette, cut into 1-inch cubes or pulled apart with a fork
- 6 tablespoons extra-virgin olive oil, divided, plus more as needed
- 1½ teaspoons flaky sea salt, divided, plus more as needed
- 2 pounds fresh ripe tomatoes, preferably a variety of colors
- 6 ounces fresh mozzarella, torn into small pieces
- ½ cup thinly sliced red onion
- 2 cloves garlic, grated
- 2 tablespoons red wine vinegar, divided, plus more as needed
- 1 tablespoon chopped fresh oregano or thyme
- Pinch of red pepper flakes
- 1 teaspoon Dijon mustard
- Freshly ground black pepper
- 1 small Persian cucumber, sliced
- ½ cup basil leaves
- ⅓ cup flat-leaf parsley leaves, roughly chopped
- ⅓ cup sliced green olives
- 6 ounces hot smoked salmon, flaked or chopped

This hearty, Italian-inspired, protein-packed herby meal of a salad features some of our favorite local ingredients and is best enjoyed when tomatoes are ripe from the garden. This salad is traditionally made without fish, but the smoked salmon adds an extra smoky, savory dimension.

Use hot smoked salmon that flakes apart, fresh mozzarella, and fresh herbs for the most flavor in every bite.

Makes 6 servings

Heat the oven to 375 degrees F. In a medium bowl, toss the bread cubes with 3 tablespoons of the oil and 1 teaspoon of the salt, then transfer to a rimmed baking sheet. Bake until the bread cubes are dry and golden at the edges, 8 to 12 minutes. Let cool on a wire rack.

Cut the tomatoes into bite-size pieces and transfer to a large bowl. Add the mozzarella, onion, garlic, 1 tablespoon of the vinegar, oregano, red pepper flakes, and ¼ teaspoon of the salt. Toss to coat and set aside.

In a medium bowl, combine the mustard, the remaining ¼ teaspoon salt, the remaining 1 tablespoon vinegar, and black pepper to taste. While whisking constantly, slowly drizzle in the remaining 3 tablespoons olive oil until the mixture is thickened. Stir in the cucumbers, basil, and parsley.

Add the bread cubes, cucumber mixture, and olives to the tomatoes and toss well. Add the smoked salmon and let sit for at least 30 minutes and up to 3 hours before serving. Toss with a little more olive oil, vinegar, and season to taste with salt before serving.

Fireweed (Hard) Lemonade

1½ cups water
½ cup freshly squeezed lemon juice
½ cup fireweed syrup (recipe follows)
1 shot (1½ ounces) fireweed-infused vodka (optional, recipe follows)
Fireweed ice cubes (recipe follows)
Mint leaves, for garnish

Fireweed blooming in late summer is a love-hate sighting for Alaskans. The magenta flowers growing tall and thick are a vision of peak season—life has exploded overhead into full color. At the same time, they're a reminder that summer won't last forever. The arrival of fireweed cues preservation season—you can eat its pink blossoms, which are mild in flavor but add color and whimsy to many dishes. Try preserving them in ice cubes, infusing vodka, or making a simple syrup for a refreshing lemonade—regular or "hard."

Makes 2 servings

To make the lemonade, in a small pitcher, mix the water, lemon juice, and syrup. For hard lemonade, add the infused vodka. Stir well to combine; chill. To serve, fill a glass with fireweed ice cubes, pour in the lemonade, and garnish with mint leaves.

1½ cups tightly packed fireweed flowers, stemmed
1 cup water
1 cup sugar
1 tablespoon freshly squeezed lemon juice

FIREWEED SIMPLE SYRUP

First, clean the flowers well by placing them in a medium bowl filled with cold water. Gently swirl the flowers with your fingers to shake loose any debris. Let the flowers sit in the water for a few minutes; scoop off any bugs or leaves. Drain the flowers.

In a medium saucepan, add the water and sugar and bring to a boil. Once boiling, add the flowers and lemon juice and boil until the color has drained from the flowers, 10 to 15 minutes. Strain the syrup through a fine-mesh strainer into a bowl. Transfer the syrup to a sealed container. Store in the refrigerator for up to 1 month.

4 cups vodka
3 cups fireweed flowers

FIREWEED-INFUSED VODKA

In a quart-size mason jar, combine 4 cups vodka and 3 cups of clean fireweed flowers. Set in a dark place and agitate the jar a few times a day for 3 to 5 days. The vodka will suck the flavor and color out of the blossoms. Strain and discard the flowers.

1 ice cube tray of water
24-36 fireweed flowers

FIREWEED ICE CUBES

Fill an ice cube tray with water. Place 2 to 3 blossoms in each cube and freeze solid.

Alaska Seafood Boil

4 quarts water
1 red onion, cut into quarters
1 whole head of garlic, cloves separated and peeled
2 pouches Old Bay or Zatarain's seafood-boil seasoning
Fresh thyme
Red or Yukon Gold potatoes, cut into 1½-inch chunks, or whole baby potatoes
Kosher salt and freshly ground black pepper
Corn on the cob, fresh or frozen
Andouille or other smoked sausage, cut into 1-inch chunks
Crab leg clusters, freshly thawed or fresh
Clams, fresh or frozen
Shrimp, fresh or frozen
Unsalted butter, melted, for serving
Lemons, for serving
Fresh parsley, for garnish

Enjoying a low-country boil with Alaskan seafood is a tradition we love and learned from our Louisiana family. Emma's husband, Jacob, grew up with crawfish boils on the weekends, and it's such a fun way to cook, eat, and bring friends and family together around the table. We like to serve shrimp, clams, and crab or other shellfish. The beautiful thing about a boil is you can improvise ingredients—whatever goes into the pot comes out tasting incredibly flavorful, so use this recipe as a guide and not a rule. Wait for a sunny day, cover a big table outside with newspaper, and wear clothes you don't mind getting messy.

Makes a feast (tailor to your desired volume)

Fill a large stockpot with the water. Add the onion, garlic, seafood seasoning, and thyme. Bring the mixture to a boil over medium-high heat.

Add the potatoes and season to taste with salt and pepper. Cook until the potatoes are almost tender, 10 to 15 minutes.

Add the corn and continue to cook for 3 minutes. Add the sausage and cook for 4 minutes longer. Add the crab and clams, cook for 3 more minutes. Add the shrimp and cook until just opaque and pink, 2 to 3 minutes.

Drain into a large colander. Arrange the seafood, vegetables, and sausage onto an extra-large serving platter or baking sheet or, if you're eating outside, spread the feast over a newspaper-covered table. Don't resist the mess, it's more delicious this way!

To finish, drizzle with the melted butter and freshly squeezed lemon juice. Sprinkle with parsley and, if you like, additional seafood seasoning and black pepper. Serve with cold beer and plenty of napkins.

VARIATIONS:

1 can of beer, to add with the water

Other herbs to add to the water, such as bay leaves or parsley

Homemade seafood seasoning (instead of store-bought)

Other seafood, such as crawfish, oysters, or lobster

Other colorful vegetables, such as green beans, okra, or asparagus

Hot sauce, for serving

Lemon Olive Oil Cake with Lemony Buttercream Frosting and Blueberries

FOR THE CAKE:
2 cups all-purpose flour
1¾ cups granulated sugar
1½ teaspoons kosher salt
½ teaspoon baking soda
½ teaspoon baking powder
1⅓ cups extra-virgin olive oil
1¼ cups whole milk
3 eggs
1 large lemon, first zested, then juiced
¼ cup Grand Marnier or other citrus liqueur

FOR THE FROSTING:
⅓ cup unsalted butter, softened
1 medium lemon, first zested, then juiced
3 cups confectioners' sugar
2 cups blueberries, for topping

This is the lemoniest cake of our dreams—zesty and sweet, light and moist. You can bake it as a single layer or divide the batter between two pans for a layer cake. We love layering the cake with buttercream frosting and topping it with fresh summer blueberries, but you might decide to use lemon curd or rhubarb sauce and dust with confectioners' sugar. It makes a great birthday cake as well as a countertop snacking cake.

Makes 1 (9-inch) cake

To make a single-layer cake, preheat the oven to 350 degrees F. Grease a 9-inch cake pan, at least 2 inches deep, with cooking spray and line the bottom with parchment paper. (If your cake pan is less than 2 inches deep, or you want to bake a layer cake, divide the batter between two 9-inch cake pans. Or, alternatively, carefully slice your cake into layers once it has baked.)

In a medium bowl, whisk together the flour, sugar, salt, baking soda, and baking powder. In a large bowl, whisk together the oil, milk, eggs, lemon zest, lemon juice, and Grand Marnier. Whisk in the flour mixture until just combined.

Pour the batter into the prepared pan and bake until the top is golden and a knife or skewer inserted in the center comes out clean, about 1 hour. (If making a double layer in two pans, bake for about 30 minutes.) Transfer the cake to a rack and let cool in the pan for 30 minutes.

Run a knife around the edge of the pan, invert the cake onto the rack and let cool completely, about 2 hours.

To make the frosting, in a medium bowl using an electric mixer, beat the butter, lemon zest, and lemon juice on medium speed for 30 seconds. Gradually beat in the confectioners' sugar. Beat the mixture until light and fluffy, about 2 minutes more.

To assemble the cake, place the cooled cake on a cake plate or stand and top with a generous layer of frosting. If making a layer cake, spread frosting between layers and on top, leaving the sides exposed. Heap blueberries on top and serve.

Fall

Wild Alaska

The sun begins to dim in the evenings, and stars are finally visible again in the night sky. A softer light illuminates the colors in nature, changing from solid green to richer golden hues. Autumn in Alaska is the season to savor the last fresh wild harvest—fat silver salmon, forest mushrooms, moose, and deer—to pick plump vegetables from the garden and berries from the bushes before the first frost hits, and to preserve the late-summer abundance and enjoy the fruits of summer's labor.

Fall is a swift season in Alaska, but the sweetest. Downshifting after the intensity of summer, coming back together with friends after a busy season, lingering and laughing over stories of adventure, and seeing familiar faces reemerge as camper vans head out of town and boats return to the harbor feels good and necessary. Fishing families are reunited and kids adjust into the familiar rhythms of school. People head back to winter work, button up summer camps and boats, put the garden to bed, and make plans to travel to warmer climates or stock the wood pile for winter. Some squeeze in a final hike into the colorful alpine, take one last plunge into the ocean, sleep outside one last time. Some gear up for their annual hunting trip with friends and family, load up into river boats or little planes, and venture out somewhere wild and quiet. Some finally get around to house projects and hope for a few more weeks of fair weather to get the job done. It seems right to be inside again, cozied up against the chill and feeling a new energy taking over. It's time to put food away, preserve, freeze, can, dry, bake, pickle, experiment with new recipes, and stock up the pantry with beautiful food for winter. Going into winter with a full freezer and loaded shelves is one of the best ways to feel prepared and resilient, no matter the weather. Brush up on canning basics, prepare your fish for the freezer, forage wild mushrooms, dry herbs, and pickle your garden harvest. Gather rose hips and make your own herbal teas and spice blends. Lean into the earthy flavors of fall and try recipes that utilize the seasonal abundance. Fall is when creativity shines—how will you preserve and share the season's flavors? Use the following traditions and recipes to live an inspired fall season.

Forage Wild Mushrooms

SUPPLIES LIST

- mushroom knife or pocketknife
- mushroom brush or clean paintbrush
- basket to collect and carry mushrooms
- mushroom identification guidebook
- GPS, map, compass for wayfinding
- waterproof clothes and boots, warm layers
- bear spray, first-aid kit, snacks, water

Gathering wild food is a great Alaskan pastime, and the early autumn season is rich with abundance. Alpine ridges and gullies are covered in berries, rivers are full of salmon, and forests and hillsides host a variety of fungi that can be safely gathered, cooked, and enjoyed. Hunting for mushrooms is both a peaceful solitary pursuit and a fun group activity. Everyone will have fun getting outside, searching for these delicious forest treasures—or "dirt meats" as some call them—and coming home to make a mushroom feast.

Mushrooms are found on forest floors from the rain forests of the Tongass National Forest to the boreal forests of the interior. August and September in Alaska are prime mushroom months, and the ideal time to forage for them is in the weeks after heavy rainfall. Mushroom gathering is allowed on most public lands for personal consumption but check with local authorities to confirm where you can harvest. Choose a spot away from roadsides, yards, or where chemicals or contaminants may be present.

Look for freshly grown young mushrooms under branches. Older, rotten mushrooms should be avoided but are a good indicator that young ones of the same variety may be nearby.

Gather only those you can clearly identify as edible. Avoid any mushrooms you are unsure about. There are a wide variety of edible Alaskan fungi; these are some of the most popular:

king bolete (*Boletus edulis*): also known as porcini, with firm, white flesh and delicious flavor

gray fire morel (*Morchella tomentosa*): found after forest fires and rain

Pacific golden chanterelle (*Cantharellus formosus*): found in Southeast Alaska

Alaskan scaber-stalk (*Leccinum alaskanum*): small bolete variety that grows under birch trees

When harvesting, pull the whole mushroom out of the ground by using your fingers to free it from the underground mycelium. This helps the mycelium grow more mushrooms. Cut off any excess stem and brush off any bugs before placing it in your basket.

Mushroom hunting can be so absorbing that it's easy to lose track of time and the distance you've wandered. Remember to keep track of the direction of your walk so you can find your way home before dark.

Back home, clean the mushrooms with a brush and cut them in half to rid them of any bugs. Prepare them immediately for cooking—sautéed in butter with a sprinkle of sea salt and fresh herbs—or slice and dry them in a dehydrator for winter soups and stir-frys.

Crab Omelet with Wild Mushrooms, Caramelized Onion, and Brie

- 2 tablespoons unsalted butter, divided
- 3 tablespoons chopped sweet onion
- ½ cup torn wild mushrooms
- ½ teaspoon flaky sea salt, plus more for seasoning
- ½ teaspoon freshly ground black pepper, plus more for seasoning
- 3 eggs
- 2 tablespoons whole milk or heavy cream
- 1 teaspoon minced parsley, plus more for garnish
- 1 teaspoon minced chives, plus more for garnish
- 3 thin slices Brie cheese
- 2 ounces (about ½ cup) crabmeat (such as king, Dungeness, or tanner)
- ⅓ cup arugula
- 1 tablespoon sour cream (optional)

Crack leftover crabmeat and save it for tomorrow's omelet. This recipe can be made with any type of crabmeat and any wild foraged or cultivated mushrooms (oysters and chanterelles are nice). Fresh herbs balance the richness of crab and Brie cheese, creating an eggy decadence you'll want to eat for breakfast, lunch, and dinner.

Makes 1 omelet

Melt 1 tablespoon of the butter in a large nonstick skillet over medium heat. Add the onion and cook until translucent. Add mushrooms and season to taste with salt and pepper. Continue cooking the onions and mushrooms, with minimal stirring, until browned and golden. Transfer to a bowl.

Crack the eggs into a small bowl. Add the milk, parsley, chives, salt, and pepper, then whisk the mixture with a fork until frothy.

Wipe out the skillet and, over medium heat, add the remaining 1 tablespoon butter, swirling the pan until the butter melts, then foams. Once the foam subsides, pour the eggs into the pan. Swirl the pan to cover the bottom with an even egg layer.

Cook the eggs over medium heat until the edges are firm and the center is just barely cooked through, 3 to 4 minutes. Deflate any large bubbles with a fork.

Lay the slices of Brie over half of the omelet. Top with the crabmeat, sprinkle with parsley and chives, and add the onions, mushrooms, and arugula.

Using a spatula, fold the omelet over on itself to form a half circle. Remove from the heat and transfer to a plate. Garnish with additional fresh herbs and a dollop of sour cream. Serve immediately.

Smoked Salmon-Chive Buttermilk Biscuits

FOR THE BISCUITS:
2 cups all-purpose flour
1 tablespoon sugar
1 tablespoon baking powder
2 teaspoons garlic powder
½ teaspoon kosher salt
¼ teaspoon cayenne (optional)
1 cup buttermilk
½ cup (1 stick) unsalted butter, melted
1½ cups shredded sharp cheddar cheese
½ cup chopped smoked salmon
¼ cup chopped chives

FOR THE TOPPING:
3 tablespoons unsalted butter, melted
1 tablespoon chopped fresh parsley leaves
½ teaspoon garlic powder

Serve up warm, cheesy, herby smoked salmon buttermilk biscuits with eggs in the morning or with a pot of soup for a simple lunch. Biscuits are a favorite food on the boat on a cold stormy day, and these are hard to stop eating with their flavorful buttery herb topping.

Makes about 10 biscuits

Preheat the oven to 450 degrees F. Grease a baking sheet.

In a large bowl, combine the flour, sugar, baking powder, garlic powder, salt, and cayenne.

In another small bowl, whisk together the buttermilk and butter. Pour the mixture over the dry ingredients and stir, using a rubber spatula, until just moist. Gently fold in the cheese, salmon, and chives.

Using a ¼-cup measuring cup, scoop the batter evenly onto the prepared baking sheet. Place in the oven and bake until golden brown, 10 to 12 minutes.

For the topping, in a small bowl, whisk together the butter, parsley, and garlic powder. Working one at a time, brush the tops of the biscuits with the butter mixture. Serve immediately.

Pumpkin Spice Pancakes

1½ cups all-purpose flour
2 tablespoons sugar
1½ teaspoons baking powder
1½ teaspoons ground cinnamon
1 teaspoon ground ginger
¾ teaspoon baking soda
¾ teaspoon kosher salt
⅛ teaspoon freshly grated nutmeg
1½ cups buttermilk
¾ cup pumpkin puree
2 eggs
3 tablespoons unsalted butter, melted, plus more for greasing the skillet
1 teaspoon vanilla extract

When the morning air crisps, bringing fall frost to the ground and changing the colors of the trees and tundra, we start craving everything pumpkin and spiced. We bring a lot of canned food on the boat with us when we're halibut fishing, since we're often far from a port with fresh fruit and vegetables. Canned pumpkin puree can be baked into a simple loaf or added to pancake mix for a special breakfast. Keep a few cans in your pantry for weekend mornings. This recipe is for pancakes from scratch—the kind that are light and fluffy with crispy, buttery edges and delicious with maple syrup and creamy maple yogurt toppings.

Makes 12 (4-inch) pancakes

In a large bowl, whisk together the flour, sugar, baking powder, cinnamon, ginger, baking soda, salt, and nutmeg until well combined.

In a medium bowl, whisk together the buttermilk, pumpkin, eggs, butter, and vanilla until well combined.

Gently fold the buttermilk mixture into the flour mixture with a rubber spatula until just combined.

Heat a lightly greased griddle or nonstick skillet over medium-low heat. Drop ¼ cup of the batter into the pan at a time, making sure to leave plenty of room between the pancakes.

Cook until the batter bubbles at the edges and browns on the bottom, 1 to 2 minutes, then carefully flip. Cook until the batter is completely cooked through and the pancakes are puffy and deep golden brown, another 1 to 2 minutes. Repeat until all the batter is used. Serve immediately.

Learn the Basics of Canning

Canning your harvest is a beautiful way to preserve your garden vegetables, wild berries, and fish and game for the winter. A batch of jam, syrup, soup, salsa, or relish in a jar makes easy and tasty meals or gifts, and there's no sweeter sight than a pantry stocked with your harvest and all your hard work. Learning the fundamentals of canning is a life skill that you'll use forever and a staple preservation method for Alaskans.

The heat of canning destroys microorganisms inside a jar and drives the air from it. As it cools, a vacuum seal is formed that prevents other microorganisms from entering and recontaminating the food. There are two methods used to preserve food in jars: the boiling water method and pressure method. Get to know the equipment needed and the basic steps for each technique.

BOILING WATER METHOD

Also known as water bath canning, this method is used for high-acid foods (like many fruits). Jars are fully submerged in boiling water for a specified time, depending on the product. The pot, with a tight-fitting cover, must be large enough for the canning jars to be completely immersed in boiling water. The jars are held off the bottom of the pot with a metal basket or rack so the heat can surround each jar evenly.

PRESSURE METHOD

Pressure canning is used for low-acid foods, such as meat and fish, which must be brought to 240 degrees F, higher than the boiling point of water, because of bacteria. This is achieved in a pressure canner, which is a heavy, steam-tight pot with a lockable lid fitted with a safety valve and vent to allow air to escape under controlled pressure. The two types of pressure canners available commercially are those with dial gauges and those with weighted gauges. It's important to keep all parts of your pressure canner clean and in good working order, because an inaccurate temperature reading can lead to underprocessed food as well as steam under high pressure (if the vent is blocked) and can be dangerous. If, for any reason, the pressure should drop during processing, the processing time must be recounted from the beginning. Follow the manufacturer's directions for the pressure canner you're using.

BREAKING DOWN THE BASICS

Regardless of the process you use, here are some guidelines for successful canning.

Choose the Right Containers

For home canning, use a heat-tempered threaded glass jar with a two-piece lid set. Regular and wide-mouth glass jars come in sizes from 4 ounces to a half-gallon and are made to seal well. Check that the rims of the jars are smooth, with no chips or cracks. The two-piece lid set consists of a flat metal lid with a rubber-like sealing compound on its underside. The other piece is a threaded metal screw band that fits over the rim of the jar and holds the lid in place. You can reuse the screw bands but not the lids. Follow the manufacturer's directions since the sealing compounds are different for each brand.

Metal cans and lids may also be used for home canning low-acid meat and fish. Alaska salmon cans are tapered and have an enamel lining appropriate for low-acid foods. A can sealer is necessary for this process.

Gather Your Tools

Helpful utensils for home canning include a jar lifter, a funnel, and a thin plastic spatula for filling jars. Knives, cutting boards, measuring spoons, and cups may be needed for making the food that you intend to process and preserve.

Prepare the Jars

Wash the jars and lids in hot, soapy water and rinse them well. Leave the jars in hot water until they're ready to use. If using a dishwasher, leave the jars in the machine until you're ready to use them.

If the processing time is less than 10 minutes, sterilize jars by submerging them in water and boiling for 10 minutes.

Pack the Jars

Pack the jars by hand or use a funnel and ladle to carefully pour the contents into each jar.

Measure Headspace Carefully

Once you've packed the jars, make sure there is enough room, known as headspace, between the top of the food or liquid and the rim of the jar. The type of food and container make a difference in the amount of headspace needed. Follow the instructions from the recipe you're using. If you overfill the jars, the contents may boil out when processed; if you leave too much headspace, a tight vacuum seal may fail to form. Too much air left inside the jar may cause the food to discolor.

Wipe Jar Tops

Use a clean, damp cloth to remove any food particles on the rims that could prevent a tight seal.

Center the Lid

With the rubber gasket side down, center the lid onto the cleaned rim of the jar. Turn the metal screw band over the flat lid until you feel slight resistance, then turn an inch more. The band should be just tight enough to hold the lid in place, but loose enough to allow the air to vent out of the jar during processing and form a vacuum seal.

Process Immediately

After jars are closed, process food right away for the exact time outlined in your recipe. Working quickly will minimize the possibility of microorganisms growing in the food.

Boiling Water Canner

Immerse the jars, closed and filled with hot food (180 degrees F) or raw food (140 degrees F) into simmering water onto the rack in the canner. Cover the pot and turn the heat to high. Start the processing time when the rolling boil begins, then maintain a gentle rolling boil for the time required. Add additional boiling water as needed to keep the tops of the jars covered by 1 to 2 inches of water. Remove the jars with a jar lifter as soon as processing time is completed and place upright on a wire rack or thick kitchen towel until cool.

Pressure Canner

With 2 to 3 inches of hot water in the canner, put filled jars with lids on the rack inside. Leave a little room so steam can surround each jar. Fasten the canner lid securely. Exhaust the canner: leave the petcock open and allow steam to escape for 10 minutes. Close the vent or place a counterweight or weighted gauge on the steam valve. When the dial gauge or weighted gauge registers the recommended pressure, start the processing time. Regulate the heat under the canner to maintain a steady correct pressure. (Follow the manufacturer's directions to learn how your weighted gauge indicates correct pressure.) When the processing time is complete, turn off the heat and let it sit until the pressure drops to zero. Remove the weight or open the petcock. Let it sit 10 minutes more, then unfasten the lid and lift it away from you as you remove it. Using a jar lifter, remove jars straight up and place on a wire rack or thick towel on the counter until cool.

AFTER CANNING

Let the jars cool at room temperature for 12 to 24 hours. Keep them out of drafts to avoid breakage. Most two-piece vacuum lids will give a "ping" as the jar seals.

After the jars have thoroughly cooled, check to see if a proper seal has occurred. Push down in the center of the lid. If it does not give, it is sealed. Remove the screw bands from the jar (it's safe to store them without the bands) and wipe the jar with a damp cloth to remove any residue. Label each jar with date and contents.

If you press the lid down and it springs up, the jar has not sealed. You can do a few things at this point. Repack the jar and use a new lid to reprocess, enjoy within 3 to 5 days, or freeze for later.

Store canned food in a cool, dry, dark place to slow the loss of nutrients. Light can accelerate oxidation, destroy certain vitamins, and fade the food's color. Properly canned food has a recommended shelf life of 1 year but it will keep indefinitely; after a year, some chemical changes tend to occur that may result in a lower-quality product.

Apple, Rhubarb, and Cranberry Chutney

- ¾ cup honey
- ½ cup red wine vinegar
- 1 tablespoon balsamic vinegar (optional)
- 2 cinnamon sticks
- 1½ tablespoons grated fresh ginger
- 1½ teaspoons orange or grapefruit zest
- ½ teaspoon ground cardamom
- ¼ teaspoon red pepper flakes
- 4 cups peeled, cored, and coarsely chopped apples
- 3 cups coarsely chopped rhubarb
- ¾ cup cranberries (dried, fresh, or frozen)
- ¼ cup chopped red onions

We became chutney people after a family friend made a giant batch to enjoy with a pig roast at Emma and Jacob's wedding. He used local apples, cranberries, and rhubarb from his yard, and it was so delicious it inspired us to start making our own. This chunky spiced preserve is good served warm, cold, or at room temperature. Store it for up to two weeks in the refrigerator. Another great option is to can a big batch of chutney to add to your pantry to enjoy later or give as gifts (see Learn the Basics of Canning, page 140). It's delicious on meat, salmon, halibut, or a simple piece of toast.

Makes about 4 cups

In a large saucepan over medium heat, combine the honey, vinegars, cinnamon, ginger, citrus zest, cardamom, and red pepper flakes; cook, stirring occasionally, until the mixture comes to a boil.

Add the apples, rhubarb, cranberries, and onions and bring back to a boil. Reduce the heat to low and simmer until the rhubarb and apples are tender but not falling apart, about 4 minutes.

Discard the cinnamon sticks in the compost and serve at your desired temperature.

Crispy Turmeric Rice with Toasted Almonds and Herbs

2½ cups water
1½ cups jasmine, basmati, or Jasmati rice, rinsed well, or 3 cups leftover cooked rice
Kosher salt
6 tablespoons (¾ stick) unsalted butter
2 tablespoons extra-virgin olive oil
¾ cup whole raw almonds, finely chopped
½ teaspoon ground turmeric
1 large shallot, thinly sliced
Freshly ground black pepper
1½ cups fresh herbs with tender stems, coarsely chopped (cilantro, mint, and/or dill are good options)

The most common meal in our fishing family's house is some variation of salmon, rice, and salad. When we have leftover rice, we love making this side dish—to enjoy again with salmon and salad! It elevates day-old grains to new heights with its golden color and flavors of earthy turmeric, buttery almonds, and abundant herbs. It's the perfect pairing to any fish, meat, or chicken.

Adapted from a recipe in Alison Roman's cookbook *Nothing Fancy*.

Makes 4 to 6 servings

In a medium saucepan, bring the water to a boil. Add the rice, salt to taste, and stir; reduce the heat to its lowest setting. Cover with a tight-fitting lid and cook until al dente, 15 to 17 minutes, or according to packaging instructions. Remove from the heat.

Heat the butter and oil in a large cast-iron or nonstick skillet over medium heat. Add the almonds and cook, stirring until toasted and the butter starts to brown, 3 to 4 minutes. Transfer the almonds to a small bowl, leaving all the butter in the pan. Season the almonds with a pinch of salt.

Add the turmeric and shallot to the skillet and season to taste with salt and pepper. Cook over medium heat, stirring occasionally, until the shallot has softened but not browned, 2 to 3 minutes. Add the cooked rice and, using a spatula or wooden spoon, press it gently into the skillet, encouraging even contact all over. Cook, without disturbing the rice, until it starts to brown on the bottom, 8 to 10 minutes. (Rotate the skillet if necessary to prevent uneven cooking and use a spatula to lift up the rice to check the progress of the browning.)

Transfer to a large serving platter, placing some of the crispier bits of rice on top, along with the fresh herbs and almonds.

Pan-Seared Scallops with Honey-Cider Glaze

- 2 tablespoons honey
- 1 tablespoon soy sauce
- 1 tablespoon Dijon mustard
- 1 teaspoon sriracha sauce
- ½ teaspoon apple cider vinegar
- ½ teaspoon freshly squeezed lime juice
- 6 large Alaska scallops
- 2 tablespoons unsalted butter
- Green onions, cilantro, or chives, chopped, for garnish

Weathervane scallops are the largest scallops in the world and the only scallops harvested commercially in Alaska. The sweet meat inside grows as big as marshmallows, and the thought of these tender morsels searing up in a pan makes our mouths water. We like to keep a bag of scallops in the freezer so we can thaw and enjoy them at ease. One of the best ways to enjoy scallops is perhaps the easiest—pan-seared in butter. Coat them in a sweet-tart glaze, sprinkle with herbs, and serve alone or over a bed of fresh tender greens.

Makes 6 scallops (about 2 servings)

In a small bowl, combine the honey, soy sauce, mustard, sriracha, vinegar, and lime juice and mix well.

Pat the scallops dry with paper towels. Melt the butter in a large skillet over medium-high heat. Add the scallops to the pan and cook until golden brown and just cooked through, about 2 minutes per side. Transfer the scallops to a large plate.

In the same skillet over medium-low heat, carefully add the honey mixture. Simmer until the mixture is reduced to a glaze, 2 to 3 minutes. Turn off the heat and quickly return the scallops to the skillet and toss well to coat with the sauce. Sprinkle with the green onions, cilantro, or chives and serve immediately.

Quick Pickle Your Garden Vegetables

TO MAKE 2 PINT JARS OF QUICK-PICKLED VEGETABLES, USE THE FOLLOWING BASIC MEASUREMENTS, OR MULTIPLY AS DESIRED:

1 pound fresh vegetables
2 sprigs fresh herbs
1 to 2 teaspoons whole spices
1 teaspoon dried herbs or ground spices
2 cloves garlic, smashed or sliced
1 cup vinegar
1 cup water
1 tablespoon kosher salt, or 2 teaspoons pickling salt
1 tablespoon sugar

Pickling at home is quick, easy, and a great way to use super fresh vegetables from your garden or farmer's market. Quick pickling is a short-term food preservation method with an acidic and delicious briny dimension, allowing vegetables to last two to three weeks in the refrigerator. This method does not require pressure cooking or canning, and you can pickle pretty much any fresh vegetable for zesty additions to recipes like tacos and salads. Experiment with slicing, peeling, or leaving ingredients whole. Some vegetables that taste delicious pickled are cauliflower, green beans, radishes, cucumbers, red onions, carrots, and cabbage. Green vegetables, such as green beans or asparagus, can be blanched in boiling water for two to three minutes then dunked in an ice bath to preserve their color before pickling, if desired.

To make quick pickles, first prepare the brine. A basic brine is equal parts vinegar and water, but you can adjust it to your preference. Any basic vinegar will get the job done, whether white, white wine, rice, or apple cider vinegar. Concentrated vinegars, like balsamic or malt vinegar, however, will not work for pickling.

- fresh herbs: dill, thyme, oregano, rosemary
- dried herbs: thyme, dill, rosemary, oregano
- garlic: smashed for mild flavor, or sliced for stronger flavor
- fresh ginger: peeled and thinly sliced
- whole spices: mustard seed, coriander, peppercorns, red pepper flakes
- ground spices: turmeric or smoked paprika add color and flavor

The trick to delicious pickled veggies is adding spices and herbs to the brine. The list to the left includes some tasty flavors that hold up well in the quick-pickle jar.

First prepare the jars. Wash the wide-mouth canning jars, lids, and screw bands you intend to use in warm, soapy water and rinse well. Set aside to dry.

Prepare the vegetables by washing, drying, peeling, chopping, and cutting into desired shapes and sizes.

Add the flavorings to the jars, dividing herbs, spices, and garlic evenly between them.

Pack the vegetables tightly into the jars, making sure there is ½ inch of headroom.

To make the brine, in a small saucepan over high heat bring the vinegar, water, salt, and sugar to a boil, stirring to dissolve the salt and sugar. Pour the brine over the vegetables, leaving ½ inch headroom.

Remove any air bubbles by tapping the jars gently against the counter a few times. Top off with more brine if necessary.

Place the lids on the jars and screw the bands on tight to seal. Let the jars cool to room temperature, then move them to the refrigerator. The flavor of the pickles will improve as they age—try waiting at least 48 hours before enjoying them.

Tinned Salmon Carbonara with Arugula and Pine Nuts

- 3 tablespoons pine nuts
- 8 ounces spaghetti
- ¼ cup diced pancetta (bacon can be used in a pinch)
- 2 whole eggs plus 1 yolk
- ½ cup grated Parmesan or pecorino Romano, plus more for serving
- 1 cup baby arugula
- 1 (6-ounce) can of wild smoked tinned salmon, drained
- Kosher salt and freshly ground black pepper

We got hooked on carbonara, the ultimate comfort food, while studying (and eating) in Italy during college. This recipe adds an Alaskan staple, smoked tinned salmon, to the traditional ingredients. If you prefer a fish-focused dish, skip the pancetta but add some olive oil to replace the rendered fat when adding the cooked pasta to the pan. The tinned salmon's great smokiness tastes incredible in a bowl of creamy pasta.

Makes 2 servings

Preheat the oven to 350 degrees F. Toast the pine nuts on a sheet pan for 5 to 10 minutes, watching closely as they tend to burn easily.

For the pasta, fill a large pot with salted water and bring to a boil. Add the pasta and cook until al dente, about 7 minutes.

While the pasta is cooking, put the pancetta in a large unheated skillet. Over medium heat, cook until the fat is rendered and the pancetta is lightly crispy, 5 to 6 minutes. Leave a couple of tablespoons of fat in the pan. (If not using pancetta, add 1 tablespoon olive oil).

Drain the cooked pasta and add it to the pancetta in the skillet over a low heat.

In a small bowl, whisk together the eggs, yolk, and grated cheese. Remove the hot skillet from the heat and fold in the egg mixture, tossing it with the spaghetti and agitating the pan to achieve a creamy texture without scrambling the eggs. Fold in the arugula, which will slightly wilt from the residual heat in the pan. With a fork, flake in the salmon. Garnish with the pine nuts, lots of fresh pepper and salt to taste, and extra grated cheese if desired.

Harvest and Dry Herbs

Planting an herb garden gives you the advantage of being able to harvest fresh herbs when you need them for cooking and also preserve them for future use. With proper storage, most dried herbs retain their flavor for about a year.

HARVEST

Herbs should be harvested when the oils responsible for their flavor and aroma are at their highest. Proper harvesting depends on the plant and how you plan to use it. Annual herbs can be cut back 50 to 75 percent and still recover. Perennial herbs can be cut back by about a third at any one time. Use a sharp knife, scissors, or pruners to make clean cuts.

Harvest early in the day after plants dry off and before they get too hot. Herbs are best harvested before they start to flower. Be careful that the plants have not been sprayed with pesticides or other chemicals.

DRY

Herbs are easy to preserve by air drying or using low heat. Drying concentrates the flavor of herbs, so you may end up only needing to use a partial amount of the fresh herbs called for in recipes. After harvesting, gently wash the herbs and dry them thoroughly on paper towels. Remove any dead or damaged parts. Tie the herbs in loose bunches to allow for good air circulation around each bunch. Place each bunch in a small paper bag and punch holes in it for ventilation. The bags help protect the herbs from dust and other contamination while drying. Hang the herb bunches in a warm, dry, well-ventilated area out of the sun. A garage, shed, barn, or well-ventilated attic work well. It may take up to a month for herbs to dry completely.

Grilled Halibut Tacos with Avocado-Cilantro Crema and Pickled Onions

You don't need a warm sunny beach to eat a good fish taco. Grilling season in Alaska lasts as long as you can stand outside without freezing, and tacos are one of our favorite ways to enjoy halibut. Its sweet, delicate flavor, snow-white flesh, and firm, flaky texture has earned it a place as the world's premium white fish, which makes halibut a candidate for the world's best fish taco. Everyone loves tacos because they hold so many flavors in each bite, and these are no exception.

Makes 4 tacos

FOR THE PICKLED ONIONS:
2 cups water
1 cup apple cider vinegar
2 tablespoons sugar
3 teaspoons kosher salt
2 red onions, thinly sliced

FOR THE CREMA:
1 ripe avocado, peeled, pitted, and flesh removed
¼ cup plain Greek yogurt
½ cup cilantro leaves and stems
1 clove garlic, minced
1 tablespoon water
1 tablespoon freshly squeezed lime juice
¼ teaspoon kosher salt

FOR THE FISH:
1 pound halibut
Kosher salt and freshly ground black pepper
2 tablespoons vegetable oil
Juice from 1 small lime
1 clove garlic, minced
1½ teaspoons chili powder
1 teaspoon ground cumin
½ teaspoon paprika
¼ teaspoon cayenne

FOR THE TACOS:
4 corn tortillas
Shredded red or green cabbage
Fresh cilantro
Cotija cheese
Hot sauce
Lime wedges for serving

To make the pickled onions, in a medium bowl, whisk together the water, vinegar, sugar, and salt until the sugar and salt dissolve. Place the onions in a jar and pour in the pickling liquid. Let the onions marinate at room temperature for 1 hour. The pickles can be made 2 weeks ahead. Store any extra in the refrigerator.

To make the crema, place the avocado, yogurt, cilantro, garlic, water, lime juice, and salt in a food processor and pulse until smooth, about 30 seconds. Cover and refrigerate.

To prepare the fish for marinating, season it with a little salt and pepper on both sides and place in a large ziplock bag.

For the marinade, in a small bowl, whisk together the oil, lime juice, garlic, chili powder, cumin, paprika, and cayenne. Pour it over the fish, seal the bag, and let it marinate for 20 to 30 minutes. ⟶

Preheat the grill to medium-high. Brush the grill grates with oil and grill the fish fillets until the center is opaque and just starts to flake, 3 to 4 minutes on each side, flipping only once (time will vary depending on the thickness of the fish). Transfer the fish to a dish and allow to rest for a few minutes before gently flaking into bite-size pieces.

Meanwhile, warm the tortillas by placing them directly on the grill and heat until just beginning to brown in spots, about 15 seconds per side.

To assemble the tacos, place halibut pieces in the center of each tortilla. Top with crema, pickled onions, cabbage, cilantro, cheese, and hot sauce, and serve with lime wedges.

STORIES FROM ALASKAN WOMEN ON TREASURED FALL FOOD TRADITIONS

"For me, the fall ritual is having the time to bake and can all the things I've spent my spring and summer collecting. Long cool evenings in the kitchen, canning the summer's sockeye, making rhubarb and huckleberry jam and beach green pesto, and baking pies. The long summer days are so busy harvesting and working, feeding the fishing crews, that when the fall comes it brings the spare time to enjoy the spoils of the summer."

—ALLIE SPURLOCK, SITKA, ALASKA (TLINGIT LAND)

"In the fall we pick highbush blueberries, moss berries, and cranberries. Our family gets together to share the catch of humpies (pink salmon), dogs (chum salmon), and other salmon that are caught in the net at the end of the runway to put up for ukla (dried fish). Brined and hung to dry with fans to keep the flies off and to dry faster. It's also a good time to put silver salmon away. We start salting salmon to make pickled fish for the winter. We make *kac'amaasaq* (half-dried fish) that we boil and eat with beach greens, boiled potatoes, and seal oil."

—CARLEEN HOBLET, FALSE PASS, ALASKA (UNANGAX̂ LAND)

Preserve Your Catch

Alaskans use many methods to preserve fish to enjoy year-round, and fall is the last chance to put your summer catch away for winter. We love frozen fish because it is quick to thaw and a tasty protein to have on hand for grilling, baking, or pan-frying through the seasons. Jars are shelf-stable, ready to enjoy with no additional cooking, and make beautiful, unique gifts as well as easy lunches.

The most important step in ensuring that your final product is delicious is careful handling of the fish after it comes out of the water. Keep the fish clean and cold, and bleed it immediately by breaking a gill with your finger or a sharp knife. Keep fish in a cooler with ice until you can dress it in a sanitary environment. Use a sharp fillet knife at a cleaning station with lots of water to gut or fillet the fish. Rinse and store the dressed fish on clean ice or in the refrigerator until you're ready to continue processing. Work quickly and carefully between harvesting and preserving to maintain maximum freshness and quality.

FREEZE FISH

To freeze fish to last a year or more, you will need access to a vacuum-packing machine. If you don't have one at home, you can rent a vacuum packer in some areas or take your fish to a processor to do this for you. You can also prepare the fish for the freezer by wrapping it first in plastic wrap and then freezer paper, but you should eat the fish soon as this method is less effective against freezer burn.

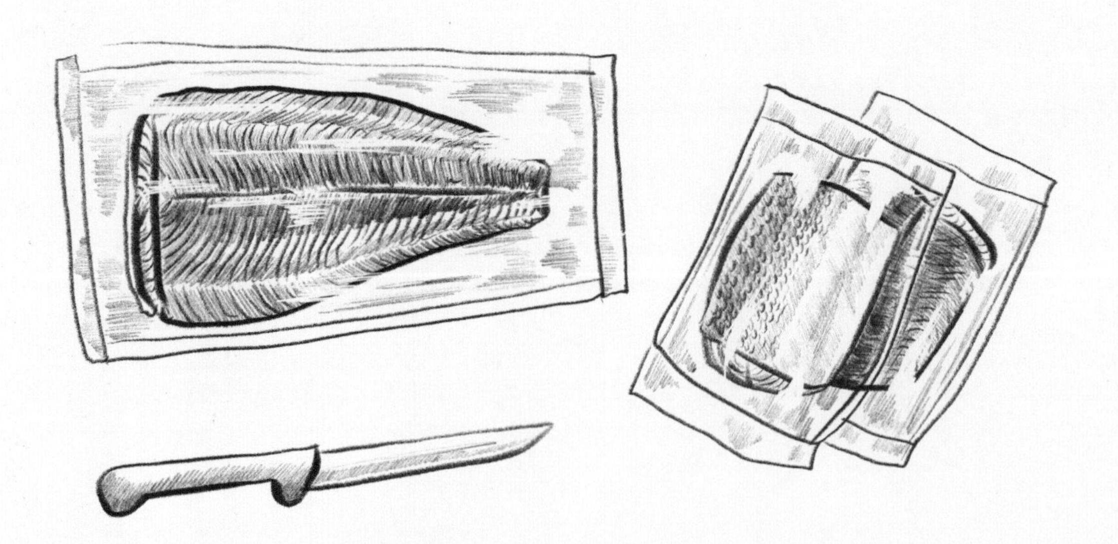

Set up an at-home packing station in your kitchen or garage with a vacuum packer, the right size vacuum seal bags for the fillets or portions of fish, paper towels to wipe away excess slime inside the bags where they will be sealed, and a permanent marker to label the contents and the date packaged before freezing.

When you place the vacuum-sealed fish in the freezer, lay the pieces out in a single layer so they can all freeze quickly. If you need to, add a temporary rack system to separate layers of fish. (Once the fish is frozen, you can remove the rack.) Set your freezer on its coldest temperature setting to maintain the quality.

JAR FISH

For most fish, remove the head, tail, and fins. It's not necessary to remove the skin, and you can leave the bones in most fish because they will soften and are a good source of calcium. When jarring halibut, remove the skin and bones, as well as head, tail, and fins.

A pressure canner is required for processing fish. The high temperatures reached under pressure are necessary to ensure a safe product. Follow the manufacturer's directions for your canner and be sure it's in good condition. Replace the gasket and safety plug if necessary and be certain the vent or petcock is clear.

Sanitize wide-mouth pint or half-pint straight-sided jars and cut the fish into jar-length fillets or chunks of any size. You can also use smoked salmon, cut into strips. If the skin is left on, you can pack the fish skin side in or out, depending on your preference. Pack solidly into jars, leaving 1 inch headspace. While no liquid or seasoning is required, you can add salt or spices for flavor. For halibut, adding ¼ cup olive oil per pint jar will add moisture to the product, if desired.

Process jars according to the manufacturer's instructions. Our recommendations for processing pint or half-pint jars of fish is 100 minutes at 10 pounds of pressure for a weighted pressure gauge and 11 pounds of pressure for a dial pressure gauge. See Learn the Basics of Canning (page 140) for more on cooling, checking the seal, and storing jars.

Sockeye Salmon Thai Red Curry with Chili Crisp

¼ cup sesame oil
1-inch piece of fresh ginger, peeled and grated
4 cloves garlic, minced or grated
2 green onions, both white and green parts, chopped, plus more for garnish
4 small shallots, chopped
1 full stalk lemongrass, finely chopped
1 cup mixed mushrooms, torn (shiitake, cremini, beech, or maitake)
3 to 4 tablespoons Thai red curry paste
2 (14-ounce) cans full-fat coconut milk
1 tablespoon fish sauce
2 teaspoons honey
1 pound wild Alaska sockeye salmon, skin removed, cut into hearty chunks
2 cups roughly chopped bok choy and/or kale
2 large limes, first zested, then juiced
¼ cup rougly chopped fresh cilantro or basil, plus more for garnish
⅓ cup roasted peanuts
Lime wedges
1 jar chili crisp
Steamed rice, such as basmati or jasmine, for serving

As the seasons change, we trade fresh salmon for fillets from our freezer. It feels so good knowing we've sealed up summer's wild nutrients with the vacuum packer and have healthy protein, omega-3s, and vitamin D on hand to brighten up the shortening days. We start cooking more warming, comforting dishes as summer becomes a memory. This Thai-inspired curry has a rich coconut milk broth and a spicy crunch, and is packed with vegetables, fresh herbs, and delicious wild sockeye salmon for a healthy fall meal.

Makes 2 to 3 servings

In a Dutch oven or large pot over medium heat, heat the sesame oil, being careful not to burn the oil. Add the ginger, garlic, green onions, shallots, and lemongrass. Cook until soft and very fragrant, 7 to 8 minutes.

Stir in the mushrooms and continue to cook until they are lightly colored and soft, another 5 minutes. Add the curry paste and mix well to coat the aromatics and mushrooms, cooking until fragrant, about 1 minute. Add the coconut milk, fish sauce, and honey and stir to combine well. Bring the mixture to a simmer and add the salmon and greens, ensuring they are submerged in the sauce. Cover the pot with a lid and cook for 4 to 5 minutes, checking the salmon for doneness. It's best to take the salmon off the heat before it's fully cooked, as the fish will continue to "carry-over cook" in the pot.

Very gently stir in the lime zest, lime juice, and cilantro or basil.

To serve, divide the rice among bowls and spoon on the curry. Garnish with peanuts, lime wedges, green onions, cilantro, and a generous spoonful of chili crisp.

Create Your Own Seasoning Blends

Turn dried garden herbs and foraged plants into your own unique seasoning blends. Having your own customized spice blends on hand is convenient, saves some money at the grocery store, and adds your own flair to your cooking. When sealed up in a glass jar, spice blends make a beautiful homemade gift to share with friends and family. If there's a combination of salts and spices you love cooking with, make it, name it something special, seal it in a glass jar, and label it.

Use the seasonal ingredients you have preserved to help guide your seasoning blends. Head out to find bulk spices at your local natural food store, and stock up on canning jars to store your blends. Here are a few of our most-cooked-with seasoning blends to inspire your own:

Furikake: with dried nori, sesame seeds, garlic, ginger, and flaky sea salt

Lemon Rosemary Sea Salt: with flaky sea salt, dried rosemary, preserved lemon, and red pepper flakes

Garden Italian: with dried oregano, basil, thyme, sage, and rosemary

In a large bowl, combine the ingredients in the desired proportions. Funnel the seasonings into glass jars, seal with a lid, and store for 6 to 12 months. Of course, they're best when they're freshest.

Gather Rose Hips

The fall, after the first frost, is the perfect time to gather rose hips, the bright-red fruit of the wild rose bush. Rose hips, like rose petals, are edible and have a tart taste and fleshy rind surrounding white seeds, which soften and sweeten after the frost hits. They are a plentiful source of vitamin C (20 to 40 percent more than an orange!) and also rich in iron, calcium, vitamin A, vitamin E, selenium, and B vitamins. Rose hips were historically consumed during fall's cold and flu season and also to prevent and treat scurvy. Today, they are often used for tea, jelly, syrup, and baked goods in Alaska. Rose hips also make beautiful decorations for the fall harvest table, or dried and strung into a garland to hang in your home.

To gather rose hips, find a patch away from busy roads or other sources of contaminants. Wear gardening gloves and bring a basket or pail and a pair of scissors or garden shears to carefully snip the hips from their prickly bushes. Once your basket is full, bring your harvest home to clean. Remove all the leaves, stems, and flowers and wash in cold water, then set the rose hips out to dry on a kitchen towel.

Use fresh rose hips to brew an immune-boosting tea. Use ¼ cup fresh hips to 1 cup boiling water. Cover and steep for 10 to 15 minutes. Strain before drinking. Add a squeeze of honey and a few mint leaves for a sweeter flavor.

You can freeze rose hips by arranging them in a single layer on a baking sheet, letting them sit in the freezer overnight, then transferring to freezer bags or containers. Rose hips will last well up to 2 years in the freezer.

You can also dry rose hips. Spread the hips on a tray in a well-ventilated room for a few days or in a dehydrator at 135 degrees F for a few hours, until crisp and brittle. We love making dried rose hip garlands by stringing up dried hips with a needle and thread.

Garlic-Butter Wild Alaska Spot Prawns with Stir-Fried Noodles

- 8 ounces rice stick noodles (fettuccine width)
- 6 tablespoons soy sauce
- ¼ cup honey
- 3 tablespoons fish sauce
- 3 tablespoons white or rice vinegar
- ½ teaspoon red pepper flakes, plus more for seasoning
- 3 tablespoons peanut or extra-virgin olive oil
- 1 pound raw wild Alaska prawns or shrimp, shell-on or peeled, deveined, and rinsed
- 3 tablespoons salted butter
- 5 cloves garlic, minced
- Pinch of freshly ground black pepper
- 3 eggs, beaten
- 2 cups bean sprouts or chopped baby bok choy
- ½ cup chopped green onions, both white and green parts
- ¼ cup toasted peanuts, chopped
- Thai basil, cilantro, and limes, for serving

We crave a big bowl of stir-fried noodles at all times. This recipe is a pad Thai–inspired combination of hot, sour, salty, and sweet flavors and crunchy, soft, chewy, and crisp textures. The key to a good bowl of home noodles is using the best ingredients available to you. We love using the wild spot prawns we catch in Prince William Sound for this dish—but any wild prawns or shrimp you have handy will taste great.

Makes 4 servings

Soak the rice noodles in hot water until they are soft and springy, about 70 percent done. (Do not boil the noodles—even if the package directions say so—or they will clump and get mushy.) Drain and toss them with a bit of sesame oil to prevent them from sticking together, set aside.

To make the sauce, in a small bowl, combine the soy sauce, honey, fish sauce, vinegar, and red pepper flakes.

Heat the oil in a large skillet over medium heat. Add the prawns and sear on both sides until pink, about 2 minutes total. Add the butter, garlic, black pepper, and a pinch of red pepper flakes. Continue to cook the shrimp until the garlic begins to caramelize and turn light golden brown, another 1 to 2 minutes.

Add the noodles and the sauce, tossing to combine. Cook until the noodles are warmed through and begin soaking up the sauce, about 1 minute. Push the noodles to one side of the skillet and add the eggs to the other. Cook until the eggs start to set, about 1 minute. Roughly scramble the eggs, then toss with the noodles. Remove from the heat. Add the bean sprouts and green onions and toss to combine.

Divide the noodles and shrimp among four plates. Top with peanuts, basil, cilantro, and red pepper flakes. Add a generous squeeze of lime juice and serve.

Chocolate Peanut Butter Pie

FOR THE CRUST:
6 tablespoons (¾ stick) unsalted butter, melted, plus more for greasing the pan
1¾ cup graham cracker crumbs
½ cup light brown sugar
½ cup unsweetened cocoa powder
½ teaspoon kosher salt

FOR THE FILLING:
1¼ cups heavy cream
1½ cups creamy peanut butter, such as Jif or Skippy
8 ounces full-fat cream cheese, at room temperature
⅔ cup light brown sugar
1 teaspoon vanilla extract
½ teaspoon kosher salt

FOR THE TOPPING (OPTIONAL):
2 ounces semisweet chocolate, chopped
1 tablespoon unsalted butter

Our family loves all things chocolate peanut butter, especially this decadent pie. Our favorite stop on the way home from our local trails is a general store that serves pieces of peanut butter pie, and it has become a tradition to stop for a post-ski piece. Make your chocolate graham cracker crust from scratch or skip this step and the oven altogether with a store-bought variety. The rest of the recipe can be completed on the stovetop and in the refrigerator, allowing a few hours to set. And then . . . silky peanut buttery–chocolatey goodness.

Makes 1 (9-inch) pie

Preheat the oven to 350 degrees F. Generously butter a 9-inch standard pie plate.

To make the crust, in a medium bowl, mix together the graham cracker crumbs, brown sugar, cocoa powder, and salt. Add the melted butter, stirring and mashing with a fork, until the crumbs are evenly moistened.

Transfer the crumbs to the prepared pan and press them evenly into the bottom and sides until the crust is about ¼-inch thick. Bake the crust until it looks dry and set, 10 to 12 minutes. Transfer the pan to a rack to cool completely, about 30 minutes.

To make the filling, in a large bowl using a handheld mixer on medium-high speed, whip the cream until stiff peaks form. Set aside. In another large bowl using the mixer on medium speed, beat the peanut butter, cream cheese, brown sugar, vanilla, and salt until fluffy, about 2 minutes. Use a large rubber spatula to gently fold the whipped cream into the peanut butter mixture. Spoon the mixture into the crust and smooth the top. Chill, uncovered, until the filling is set, 4 to 6 hours.

To make the topping, in a microwave-safe bowl, melt the chocolate and the butter together in short bursts, stirring often. Transfer the chocolate mixture to a small plastic bag and cut a ⅛-inch hole in one corner. Drizzle the chocolate over the top in a decorative pattern. Serve immediately or cover and refrigerate for later.

Make Your Own Herbal Tea

Making your own tea blends suited to your taste and needs can give your body, mind, and spirit a gentle boost. Use herbs and flowers you have grown or collected, or source from a local natural foods store to ensure quality, fresh taste, and nutritional value. We love the idea of collecting plants local to your area to make a tea that tastes of your home—a portrait of a place, in your cup!

Mixing your own herbs for tea is easy—choose your favorite scents or select herbs based on their benefits. Fall is an ideal time to round out your tea selection with immune-boosting herbs, before cold and flu season arrives along with chilly weather.

Though there are no rules to making your own tea blends, a good herbal tea provides a range of tastes. Try this basic recipe:

1 part floral flavor: Fresh or dried flower petals, including nasturtiums, violet flowers, chamomile flowers, yarrow, dandelion petals, wild rose petals, fireweed blossoms, salmonberry blossoms, or Labrador tea.

2 parts base flavor: Something to tie everything together. Try dried red raspberry leaves or dried nettles.

1 part fruity flavor: Add a naturally sweet component like dried rose hips, blueberries, or green apple.

1 part cooling herb: Try mint, lemon balm, neem, or borage to finish.

Mix all the herbs together and store in an airtight container. To brew, use a tea ball to steep 1 teaspoon of the tea blend in hot water for 6 to 8 minutes.

Salmon
Sisters
Harvested, smoked
& packed in Alaska

FALL EQUINOX FEAST

MENU

Harvest Moon Old Fashioned
page 173

Seafood Charcuterie Board
page 175

Tomato Soup with Basil Pesto
page 176

Black Cod with Kale and Wild Mushrooms over Creamy Grits
page 179

Orange and Rosemary Upside-Down Cake
page 183

In late September, the autumn equinox marks the official end of summer and the beginning of fall in the northern hemisphere. Equinox means “equal night,” and most places on Earth will see about twelve hours of daylight and twelve hours of darkness on this date. In Alaska, the equinox marks the end of the harvest season and is the perfect occasion to gather for a harvest feast. Bundle up in your warmest sweater and find a location amidst fall’s glowing colors to set a table for a final meal together outdoors. Add rose hips, golden grasses, or other colorful fall foliage to the table, pull candles out of the cupboard, and assemble a charcuterie board of seafood as the table’s centerpiece. Greet guests with spiced cocktails, made with fresh-pressed apple cider, and serve a hearty meal of homemade creamy tomato soup swirled with fresh pesto, rich black cod with garden greens and fall mushrooms, and an after-dinner slice of citrus rosemary cake. Wind down together, invite your friends and family to bring something from their garden or pantry to contribute, and celebrate the fruits of summer’s labor.

Harvest Moon Old Fashioned

4 ounces bourbon
1 ounce pure maple syrup
1 ounce apple cider
4 dashes of angostura bitters
Ice
Freshly grated nutmeg, for garnish
2 cinnamon sticks, for garnish

Celebrate the autumn equinox with a crisp apple cider and maple syrup old fashioned, the perfect cocktail for a cozy fall gathering. You can make it a mocktail by swapping out the bourbon for brewed black tea, which has a similar earthy, bitter flavor. Cheers to a slower season.

Makes 2 servings

Divide the bourbon, syrup, cider, and bitters between rocks glasses. Fill the glasses with ice and stir until cold. Garnish each with grated nutmeg and a cinnamon stick.

STORIES FROM ALASKAN WOMEN ON CELEBRATING THE FALL

"I celebrate the fall with the return of my fishing sweetheart and friends, by having salmon canning parties, and dinners with everything homemade!"

—ALLIE SPURLOCK, SITKA, ALASKA (TLINGIT LAND)

"Like many Alaskans, my family eagerly waits until after the second or third hard frost for our annual carrot harvest day. Each cold night drives more sugar to the root, and each cold morning promises more sweetness, more delicious potential. We fill a wheelbarrow with the best, most cylindrical, a basket with the oddly shaped and smallest, and a large bin with the still-green tops. All three will nourish us in different ways throughout the winter. The near-perfect, straight ones we store—promising crunch and juicy freshness in January. The multilegged and small ones land in the kitchen later in the day, where we turn them into sauerkraut. Last, we puree the bright-green tops and make a vibrant pesto that tastes like grassy long summer days when the garden is asleep under snow."

—EVIE WITTEN, ANCHORAGE, ALASKA (DENA'INA LAND)

"We spend a lot of time preparing our fresh catches to enjoy together, whether it's in the kitchen or outside over a bonfire or grill. We celebrate over fresh mossberry pie, over pickled salmon, or over fresh salmon heads wrapped in putchki leaves. Fall is one giant celebration, but there's also lots of work to do!

—MARIA DOSAL, KING COVE, ALASKA (UNANGAX̂ LAND)

Seafood Charcuterie Board

Create an epic spread with delicacies from the sea like tinned fish, smoked salmon strips, caviar, oysters, and kelp pickles. This fish-forward charcuterie makes an incredible appetizer or snack board for any small gathering—just draw from ingredients in your pantry and look for tasty additions at your local fish market or specialty food stores. Find a large wooden board and arrange with bowls of various sizes to hold spreads and more unruly ingredients. Place tins of fish directly on the board along with vegetables, fruits, cheeses, dips, pickles, condiments, breads, and crackers. Get creative and use fun little mismatched forks and spoons for serving with a pile of napkins or small plates.

FOR THE MAIN INGREDIENTS:

- Sliced salmon lox
- Hot smoked fish (whitefish or salmon)
- Seafood in their tins (such as salmon, octopus, herring, sardines, or smoked oysters)
- Fresh oysters on the half shell
- Pickled kelp
- Pickled vegetables
- Heirloom tomatoes
- Colorful carrots
- Half rounds of soft cheeses
- Sliced local cheeses
- Marinated white beans
- Olives
- Grapes
- Apples
- Almonds, pistachios, or other salty nuts
- Preserved lemon

FOR THE SPREADS:

- Marinated goat cheese
- Smoked fish dips
- Fish pâtés
- Caviar
- Jams, chutneys, preserves
- Grainy mustard

FOR THE ACCOMPANIMENTS:

- Torn pieces of crusty bread
- Rustic crackers
- Flatbreads
- Pita chips

Creamy Tomato Soup with Basil Pesto

- 1 tablespoon extra-virgin olive oil
- 2 large carrots, finely diced
- 1 small yellow onion, finely diced
- 3 ribs celery, finely diced
- 4 cups low-sodium chicken broth
- 2 (14.5-ounce) cans diced tomatoes, undrained
- 2 tablespoons tomato paste
- 1½ teaspoons dried basil
- 1 teaspoon dried oregano
- ¼ cup unsalted butter
- ¼ cup all-purpose flour
- 1½ cups half-and-half or whole milk
- 1 cup freshly grated Parmesan cheese
- ¼ cup chopped fresh basil
- 1 teaspoon kosher salt
- ¼ teaspoon freshly ground black pepper
- Basil pesto, for serving
- Crusty bread, for serving

Perfect fall-weather comfort food means creamy tomato soup from scratch with a swirl of basil pesto in your bowl. This soup—thickened with a roux, not cream—picks us up when a day feels stormy, and it warms us up after a day of doing projects outdoors.

Makes 4 to 6 servings

Heat the oil in a large pot over medium-high heat. Add the carrots, onion, and celery and cook for a few minutes until they begin to sweat.

Add the broth, tomatoes with their juice, the tomato paste, basil, and oregano. Bring to a gentle boil and cook for several minutes, until the vegetables are tender. Use an immersion blender to puree the soup until smooth.

To prepare the roux (flour mixture), melt the butter in a medium saucepan over medium-low heat. Stir in the flour and whisk constantly until the roux turns golden brown, about 10 minutes.

Add a big ladleful of the soup to the roux—it will start to form a thick paste. Add a few more big scoops of soup to the roux and stir well until smooth. Add the roux mixture to the tomato mixture and stir to combine.

Stir in the half-and-half, Parmesan cheese, fresh basil, salt, and pepper. If you like, add additional dried oregano or basil to taste. Cook for a few more minutes until warmed through.

Swirl a big spoonful of basil pesto into the middle of each bowl of soup and serve with crusty bread for dunking.

Black Cod with Wild Mushrooms and Kale over Creamy Grits

FOR THE GRITS:
4½ cups water
2 cups whole milk
1 teaspoon kosher salt
2 cups grits, polenta, or cornmeal
¼ cup unsalted butter
1 tablespoon grated Parmesan

FOR THE MUSHROOMS:
4 ounces fresh wild mushrooms, such as morel, shiitake, trumpet, or hedgehog
2 tablespoons neutral oil, such as grapeseed or vegetable
¼ cup unsalted butter
2 sprigs fresh thyme
Kosher salt and freshly ground black pepper

FOR THE KALE:
1½ tablespoons extra-virgin olive oil
1 medium yellow onion, diced
4 cloves garlic, minced
1 bunch kale, stemmed, leaves chopped
2 cups water
2 tablespoons white vinegar
Kosher salt and freshly ground black pepper

Our family's boats and crew go to sea to harvest black cod, also known as sablefish, in the fall. Their season ends in November, and we always look forward to hearing their stories of big storms, pots full of fish, and wild scenery upon their return. The rich, oily flavor of black cod is an Alaskan delicacy, and enjoying this fish over creamy grits with wild foraged mushrooms and greens from the garden makes for a true harvest feast.

Makes 4 servings

To make the grits, in a heavy medium saucepan over medium-high heat, bring the water and milk to a high simmer. Add the salt. Slowly pour in the grits, stirring with a wire whisk to prevent any clumping. Continue stirring often as the mixture thickens, 2 to 3 minutes.

Turn the heat to low and cook for 40 to 45 minutes, stirring every 5 to 10 minutes. If the grits become too thick, thin with ½ cup water and continue cooking, adding more water as necessary to keep the grits soft enough to stir. Add the butter and Parmesan, taste, and adjust the seasoning to your liking.

Meanwhile, clean the mushrooms with a damp towel, then slice them. Heat the oil in a large sauté pan over medium-high heat. Add the butter and thyme and stir with a wooden spoon, watching carefully to ensure the butter doesn't burn. When the butter is melted, add the mushrooms and sear until golden brown. Season to taste with salt and pepper.

To prepare the kale, heat the oil in a large pot over medium-high heat. Add the onion and garlic and cook for 5 minutes, stirring occasionally. Add the kale, water, vinegar, and salt and pepper to taste. Cook, stirring occasionally, until the liquid is mostly evaporated. Keep warm until ready to serve. ⟶

FOR THE FISH:
4 (4-ounce) fillets skin-on black cod
Kosher salt and freshly ground black pepper
1½ tablespoons extra-virgin olive oil, plus more for garnish
Freshly squeezed lemon juice, for garnish

To cook the fish, place a heavy-bottom or cast-iron sauté pan over high heat for 5 minutes. Pat the fillets dry with a paper towel. Season both sides lightly with salt and pepper. Add the oil to the pan and place the fish skin side down. Sear the fillets for about 4 minutes, reducing the heat if the oil starts to burn, then flip them over. Turn off the heat and let the fish cook in the pan to your preferred doneness, being careful not to overcook, about 2 minutes more. Drain the fillets on paper towels.

To serve, dish up servings of grits onto plates and top with the kale, mushrooms, and portions of black cod. Drizzle with some high-quality extra-virgin olive oil and lemon juice.

STORIES FROM ALASKAN WOMEN ON THRIVING IN FALL

"Embrace the change of seasons. Though summer may be over, it's nearly time to pick mushrooms, bake cakes and pies, or prepare your trapline. For many here on my island, it's time to play music and make art as well!"

—ALLIE SPURLOCK, SITKA, ALASKA (TLINGIT LAND)

"Be willing to put the work in and show up with your boots on! Also, have enough jars on hand for your berries and fish, you're going to need them!"

—MARIA DOSAL, KING COVE, ALASKA (UNANGAX̂ LAND)

"For me, fall is a time for grounding and gathering, and to celebrate the brief season of balanced day and night in the North. It's a time to welcome back the stars and to take long hikes in brisk air, seeking out the earthy, umami scent of highbush cranberries (*Viburnum edule*) and plump rose hips. Most importantly, fall is a time to gather with dear ones around the table, all of us ready to be nourished by our harvests and our stories of summer work and adventures and grateful for the strength that comes from kinship and shared lives."

—EVIE WITTEN, ANCHORAGE, ALASKA (DENA'INA LAND)

Orange and Rosemary Upside-Down Cake

FOR THE ORANGES:

1 cup water
1 cup sugar
3 blood oranges or other brightly colored orange, rinsed, scrubbed, and ends removed
1 medium sprig fresh rosemary, plus a few finely chopped needles (optional)

FOR THE CAKE:

1½ cups all-purpose flour
2 teaspoons baking powder
¾ cup sugar
⅓ cup unsalted butter, at room temperature
2 eggs, separated
2 teaspoons vanilla extract
½ teaspoon freshly grated nutmeg
⅓ cup plus 1 tablespoon whole milk
⅛ teaspoon fine sea salt

The smell of oranges and sprigs of rosemary simmering on the stovetop is enough to inspire anyone to make this aromatic cake. It is arranged from bottom up and baked in parchment paper, which, when peeled back, reveals a lovely arrangement of caramelized orange slices.

Makes 1 (8-inch) cake

Preheat the oven to 350 degrees F. Line an 8-inch springform pan with parchment paper.

To make the oranges, in a large saucepan over medium-high heat, bring the water and sugar to a boil. Stir until the sugar dissolves. Cut the oranges into ⅛-inch slices. Reduce the heat to medium, layer the orange slices in the sugar water, and simmer gently for 25 to 30 minutes, or until the oranges are soft but retain their shape. Using a slotted spoon, transfer the orange slices to a large plate and let them cool. Add the rosemary sprig to the saucepan with the orange syrup and set aside.

To make the cake, in a medium bowl, combine the flour and baking powder. In the bowl of a stand mixer fitted with the paddle attachment, beat the sugar and butter until light and fluffy, 2 to 3 minutes. Add the egg yolks, vanilla, and nutmeg and continue mixing until well combined, about 1 minute. Quickly add the flour mixture in three parts, alternating with the milk, starting and ending with the flour. Transfer batter to a large mixing bowl and set aside.

Wash and dry the mixer bowl. Fit the mixer with the whisk attachment and beat the egg whites and salt until soft peaks form. Fold the egg whites into the batter.

Arrange the orange slices on the bottom and along the sides of the prepared pan, folding some of the slices into the corners. Spoon the batter on top of the sliced oranges and even it out with a rubber spatula. Bake the cake until golden brown and spongy and a skewer or knife inserted in the center comes out clean, 35 to 40 minutes. Let the cake cool on a rack for 10 minutes, then invert it and gently remove the parchment paper.

Bring the orange syrup to a boil over high heat and cook for about 2 minutes. Remove from the heat and let cool. Brush the top of the cake with the syrup and arrange the rosemary sprig as a centerpiece. Sprinkle the cake with chopped rosemary, slice, and enjoy.

Winter

Winter in the North is a long season of little daylight. A whole day can be filled up with simple tasks like shoveling snow and bringing firewood inside. There are no "quick" trips to town for errands–instead, any outing involves heating up the car and shoveling the driveway, bundling up in all the layers and snow boots, driving slowly through snow and ice, and making room for moose wandering into town to escape the deep drifts. Things take time. Time slows down. Winter lets us take a breath and rest. Everything moves slower and the world quiets under a cold blanket of snow and ice. Eyes closed, we turn our faces to the sky, soaking up as much vitamin D as possible and counting down to the winter solstice and the return of the light. "We made it" is a common phrase repeated this time of year.

Embracing winter in all of its extremes is necessary to its enjoyment. The first snow is a signal to slow down and rest after the hustle and bustle of summer adventure and fall harvest. A stormy day may be a sign to stay inside and bake a loaf of sourdough and start a pot of stew instead of maintaining your normal busy routine. A magical, cold clear day may invite you to bundle up in your warmest gear and take your family ice fishing or out into the woods on snowshoes or skis. Living seasonally means constantly adjusting expectations for what a day looks like, and in winter it means giving yourself the space to go slower and savor solitude, reflection, and creativity while the light is low and the world is quiet.

Something about the cold makes the holidays feel extra bright and necessary. We are grateful for a reason to celebrate, come together, and enjoy each other's company around the table and outside in winter. This is the season when all the summer and fall harvest tucked away in the pantry feels like riches. The taste of a tin of smoked salmon brings us back to the 10 p.m. sunshine sparkling across the sea and the smell of a driftwood campfire. A jar of jam transports us to our happy place deep in a blueberry patch, fingers busy as our minds drift on the tundra breeze. Sweet shrimp in the freezer remind us of the soft burn of the line coiling in our hands and the smell of fresh, rich mud from the deep. Sharing a bountiful harvest is one of life's great joys in Alaska because of the stories that come with it.

Nutty Cinnamon Banana Smoothie

- 1 banana, frozen or fresh
- ½ cup almond or oat milk
- 2 generous tablespoons almond or peanut butter
- 2 tablespoons plain Greek yogurt
- 1 tablespoon agave or honey
- Sprinkle of cinnamon

A creamy, nutty, spiced smoothie built with good-for-you, warming ingredients perfect for the winter season. This recipe is inspired by a drink we order from a coffee stand on our 220-mile road trip from our seaside town to the city. It's a delightful treat to savor on the highway (with whipped cream!) or at home for breakfast or an afternoon snack.

Makes 1 serving

Place the banana, milk, nut butter, yogurt, and sweetener in a blender. Cover and blend until smooth. Top with a sprinkle of cinnamon. If you prefer your smoothie cold, use a frozen banana or add a few ice cubes. Enjoy immediately.

STORIES FROM ALASKAN WOMEN ON TREASURED WINTER FOOD TRADITIONS

"I love my relatively new food ritual which revolves around my fellow free-diving Seldovia moms—we spearfish for greenling, and whatever else we are lucky enough to spear or forage. We coordinate and decide which location will be the best choice, taking into consideration the tide, wind, and winter temperatures. It's too cold for a beach fire after the worst of winter, so if we are successful, we choose whose house we will meet at, and after a warm shower, we have an amazingly fresh meal of tacos. We are a mixed bunch of women and of all experience levels, but we look forward to each time we get in the water together."

—JANEL HARRIS, SELDOVIA, ALASKA (ALUTIIQ, UNANGAX̂, DENA'INA LAND)

"We love to slow down and enjoy our bounty from the hectic summer months. Berries that we picked and froze are used to make sweet treats until we can pick again. Hot stews using the caribou and black bear my husband and daughter harvested together. Sourdough bread topped with our smoked salmon and homemade cheese. All our hard work can be enjoyed for several months together as we make plans for the upcoming season!"

—LISA HARLOW, FAIRBANKS, ALASKA (TANANA LAND)

Grow Bulbs Indoors

Growing bulbs inside your home lets you enjoy the lively fragrance of spring when it's still months away. Amaryllis and paperwhite narcissus are two types of bulbs that are native to warm climates and don't require a cooling period to trigger blooms, which makes them easy to grow inside at room temperature. Find bulbs at your local garden store.

Amaryllis bulbs are best planted in a pot filled with soil, with about a third of the bulb above the soil line. Place in bright, indirect light and water sparingly until growth begins. Amaryllis are available in many interesting colors and forms and in scents that range from delicate and mild to sweet.

Paperwhite bulbs can be planted or just placed in a shallow bowl with pebbles to hold the bulbs in place. Add enough water to cover no more than the bottom third of the bulb, and they will usually bloom around four weeks after planting. Paperwhites have white petals and an intense, delicious fragrance.

Smoked Salmon Strata with Goat Cheese and Dill

- ¼ cup unsalted butter, softened, plus 3 teaspoons, divided
- 12 slices white bread
- 8 eggs, divided
- ½ cup plus 2 tablespoons whole milk, divided
- ¼ teaspoon kosher salt
- ¼ teaspoon freshly ground black pepper
- Dash of freshly grated nutmeg
- Dash of cayenne
- 1 cup firm goat cheese, crumbled, divided
- ½ cup sun-dried tomatoes (not oil-packed), chopped
- ½ cup chopped leeks, white and light-green parts, washed thoroughly
- 6 ounces smoked salmon or lox, cut into thin strips, plus more for garnish
- 1 tablespoon chopped fresh dill, or 1 teaspoon dried dill, plus more for garnish

A savory egg bake for a winter weekend morning, brunch with friends, or holiday breakfast. Start this recipe the night before, refrigerate overnight, and in the morning just pop the dish in the oven and bake. The smoked salmon gives this strata a savory, smoky, salty bite balanced out by the creamy eggs and goat cheese, bright, fresh ingredients, and comforting hint of nutmeg.

Makes 4 to 6 servings

Use 2 teaspoons of the butter to grease a 13-by-9-inch baking dish or 10-inch cast-iron pan. Lightly spread the ¼ cup softened butter on both sides of the bread slices. Cut the slices diagonally in half. Line the sides of the dish with about 9 bread triangles, overlapping them slightly with long edges down. Line the bottom of the dish with about 8 bread triangles, cutting to fit as necessary. Reserve the remaining bread triangles.

In a small bowl, whisk together 5 of the eggs, ½ cup of the milk, the salt, pepper, nutmeg, and cayenne. Drizzle about ⅓ of the egg mixture over the bread slices in the bottom of the dish. Reserve the remaining egg mixture.

In another small bowl, whisk together the remaining 3 eggs and 2 tablespoons milk and set aside for the next step.

Melt the remaining 1 teaspoon butter in a small skillet over medium heat. Add the egg mixture and stir with a wooden spoon until the eggs are softly scrambled. Remove from the heat and spread the eggs over the bread slices. Sprinkle evenly with ½ cup of the goat cheese, the sun-dried tomatoes, leeks, smoked salmon, and dill.

Arrange the reserved bread slices in a single layer over the top and drizzle with the reserved egg mixture. Sprinkle the remaining goat cheese evenly over the bread. Cover and refrigerate overnight (along with the remaining smoked salmon).

Preheat the oven to 375 degrees F.

Let the chilled strata stand at room temperature while the oven preheats. Place the strata on a baking sheet to catch any overflow. Bake until the top of the strata is golden, 40 to 45 minutes. Remove from the oven and cool for 5 minutes. Garnish with fresh dill and smoked salmon pieces and serve.

Stock Your Pantry with Staples

Cooking is simpler and faster when you already have the ingredients on hand. Stock your pantry and freezer with staples that last and can be relied upon. Start fresh by taking everything out of your pantry and get rid of anything you haven't used in a year. Keep what smells and looks good and organize your shelves or freezer according to logic that makes sense to you. Fill any empty shelves with food that you like and inspires you to cook. Here are some tips and a list of things we like to have on hand in our kitchen and on our boat—we only need to add one or two fresh ingredients to cook most recipes from scratch.

TIPS FOR ORGANIZING

Make everything visible so you can see what you have and what you're running low on. A storage space with plenty of shelving is the most efficient configuration for ingredients.

Store everything in clear, airtight containers, like large jars or rectangular plastic Tupperware.

Keep a roll of masking tape and Sharpies handy to make quick labels.

TIPS FOR REDUCING WASTE AND MAXIMIZING INGREDIENTS

Be realistic about your habits. Buy smaller quantities of fresh things you don't use as often.

Buy ground spices in the smallest quantities you can find, except for spices you use regularly.

Buy fresh herbs. Many dried herbs lose flavor quickly in storage.

Buy heavy, shelf-stable ingredients like boxed broth and canned foods in bulk or order them online to save time and effort.

Cook anything in your refrigerator that looks tired, even if you're not sure what you'll make with it yet. You can always throw it into a salad or pasta or a grain bowl.

PANTRY ESSENTIALS:

oils and vinegars: extra-virgin olive oil, neutral cooking oil (vegetable or grapeseed), sesame oil, coconut oil, red wine vinegar, white vinegar, white wine vinegar, apple cider vinegar, balsamic vinegar

cans and jars: tinned fish (salmon, sardines, anchovies), tomato paste, diced tomatoes, tomato sauce, chicken and/or vegetable stock, canned beans (white, black, and/or chickpeas), black olives, unsweetened coconut milk

spices and dried herbs: kosher salt, flaky sea salt, red pepper flakes, cayenne, curry powder, bay leaves, black peppercorns, paprika, ground cinnamon, ground nutmeg, ground cumin, garlic powder, dried thyme, dried oregano

grains and starches: rice (white and brown), quinoa, dried pasta (long noodles and short pasta shapes), rice noodles, plain bread crumbs, crackers, dried lentils and beans, shelf-stable tofu, corn grits, tortillas

nuts and nut butters: walnuts, almonds, pecans, roasted peanuts, peanut butter, almond butter

sweeteners: honey, maple syrup, granulated sugar

preserves and pickles: fruit jams and preserves, pickles, pickled beets and/or other vegetables, olives

condiments and sauces: vinaigrette, mustard (yellow or Dijon), mayonnaise, ketchup, hot sauce, salsa, soy sauce, Thai red curry paste, fish sauce, Worcestershire sauce, teriyaki sauce, miso paste

produce: garlic, onions, potatoes (all-purpose and sweet), lemons, carrots, celery, ginger

dairy: eggs, butter, cheeses (cheddar, Jack or Colby, pecorino or Parmesan, feta), milk or cream for cooking, plain full-fat yogurt

freezer: fish fillets, chicken, sausages, ground meat, shrimp, fish stock, thick-sliced bread (for toast), spinach (and other vegetables such as corn and peas), berries (and other fruit such as mango and peaches)

baking: all-purpose flour, whole wheat flour, cornmeal, rolled oats, cornstarch, baking soda, baking powder, pure vanilla extract, brown sugar, confectioners' sugar, bittersweet baking chocolate, chocolate chips, dried fruit, cocoa powder, active dry yeast, evaporated milk

drinks: tea (black, green, and herbal), coffee, chai, hot chocolate

Creamy Steel-Cut Oats with Maple Applesauce and Walnuts

FOR THE OATS:

2 teaspoons unsalted butter
1 cup steel-cut oats
3 cups whole milk
1 cup water
½ teaspoon kosher salt

FOR THE APPLESAUCE:

2 large apples, peeled or unpeeled, cored, and roughly chopped
2 tablespoons maple syrup
1 tablespoon water
½ teaspoon ground cinnamon
¼ teaspoon kosher salt
¼ teaspoon ground nutmeg
A few grinds of freshly ground black pepper

FOR THE TOPPING:

Toasted walnuts, chopped
Toasted coconut flakes
Plain Greek yogurt
Heavy cream

Elevate your oats with stewed apples, maple sweetness, cinnamon, and nutty crunch. Make the applesauce as your pot of oats cook and surprise even the most uncertain oatmeal eaters with a warming bowl of flavor. We love steel-cut oats for their texture, but if you're looking for something quicker, rolled or instant oats work well too. The theory behind a good bowl of oatmeal, in our opinion, is loading it up with as many delicious ingredients as possible. Try this recipe, and then improvise with whatever you have in the pantry—frozen berries, nut butters, seeds, nuts, crunchy granola, dried or fresh fruit, compotes, jams, syrups—or go wild and go savory!

Makes 4 servings

To make the oats, melt the butter in a medium saucepan over medium-high heat. Stir in the oats and cook until toasty, 2 to 3 minutes. Stir in the milk, water, and salt and bring to a boil. Reduce to a simmer and cook, stirring frequently, for about 25 minutes.

To make the applesauce, in a small saucepan, combine the apples, maple syrup, water, cinnamon, salt, nutmeg, and pepper and bring to a boil; reduce the heat. Simmer until the apples are very tender, about 15 minutes. Using an immersion blender or a food processor, blend the apples until smooth, or leave them chunky for a more rustic texture.

To serve, divide the oatmeal among bowls. Top with the applesauce, walnuts, coconut, a dollop of yogurt, and a dash of cream.

Light up the Night with Ice Lanterns

SUPPLIES LIST

- a few large buckets or containers
- a few smaller buckets or containers
- a few rocks or weights
- a few small planks
- pine sprigs, berries, rose hips, or other decorations (optional)
- candles

Light up dark winter nights and invite guests in with the magical glow of an ice lantern along your walkway or porch. Ice lanterns are a tradition among northern cultures where daylight is short. Historically, they served as beacons on fishing boats and lamps on paths and streets of villages and are part of the Scandinavian holiday tradition of lighting up the shortest day of the year, winter solstice. Making ice lanterns is easy. You just need a few simple tools—and below-freezing temperatures outside. You can create ice lanterns in many shapes and sizes and even add greenery or other decorations. Depending on the weather, they'll last for days.

Fill a large bucket with water to within a few inches from the top.

Put a rock or weight in a smaller bucket and place it in the large bucket of water, making sure it doesn't tip over. If you like, add decorations to the water around the small bucket, such as pine sprigs or berries.

Place a plank or piece of wood across the top of the buckets to hold the smaller bucket in place in the center of the large bucket. Place another rock or weight on top of the plank to keep everything in place.

Set the buckets to freeze outside overnight, or until solid.

Disassemble the buckets and pop the ice lanterns out. If they are difficult to remove, pour a little hot water on top to help loosen the edges.

Arrange the lanterns outside, well side up. Place a candle in each icy well, light the candles carefully, and watch the lanterns glow!

Crispy Smashed Potatoes with Salmon Caviar

FOR THE WHIPPED GOAT CHEESE:

8 ounces plain goat cheese, softened
3 tablespoons whole milk
2 tablespoons sour cream
2 tablespoons minced shallot
1 tablespoon chopped fresh herbs, such as dill or chives
½ grapefruit or lemon
Kosher salt and freshly ground black pepper

FOR THE SMASHED POTATOES:

8 ounces slab or thick-cut bacon, large diced
1 tablespoon extra-virgin olive oil, plus more for drizzling
12 baby Yukon gold potatoes or comparable variety
1 tablespoon kosher salt, plus more for seasoning
Freshly ground black pepper
1 avocado, peeled, pitted, and sliced
1 green onion, white and green parts, chopped
Fresh herbs, such as dill or cilantro
1 (1.75-ounce/50-gram) jar salmon caviar (smoked, if available)
Extra-virgin olive oil, for garnish

We cure and eat roe regularly in the summer when the salmon are running and we're living on the water. Salmon roe—or caviar—becomes rarer in the winter months without immediate access to it. Some Alaskan processors smoke and jar caviar, and it's one of our favorite products to stock in our shops and pantries. This indulgent dish pairs the salty bursts of salmon caviar with the comforting pleasure of smashed baked potatoes. Serve this as an appetizer or a celebratory side dish with your favorite seafood, meat, or vegetables.

Makes 4 to 6 portions

To make the whipped goat cheese, place the cheese in the bowl of a stand mixer fitted with the paddle attachment. Whip until light and fluffy, then add the milk, sour cream, and shallots and continue to mix. Add the herbs, a good squeeze of grapefruit or lemon juice for acidity, and season to taste with salt and pepper. Set aside at room temperature.

To make the potatoes, place the bacon in a cold skillet with 1 tablespoon of oil and cook over medium heat until the bacon is crispy, about 10 minutes. Remove the bacon from the pan and drain on paper towels in a warm place.

In a large pot, add the potatoes, salt, and enough water to fully cover the potatoes. Bring to a boil over high heat, then reduce the heat to medium and simmer the potatoes until a knife can pierce them easily, 20 to 25 minutes.

Preheat the oven to 400 degrees F.

Drain the potatoes in a colander and allow them to let off steam for 5 minutes. Spread the potatoes on a parchment-paper-lined sheet pan and use the bottom of a mason jar or masher to smash the potatoes until about ½ inch thick. The thinner they are, the crispier they'll get! Let them rest for an additional 5 minutes. Drizzle the potatoes with oil (and bacon grease, if desired) and generously season with salt and pepper. Bake until golden brown, or until the desired crispiness is reached, 40 to 50 minutes.

Garnish the potatoes with the whipped goat cheese, avocado, green onion, fresh herbs, a healthy spoonful of caviar, and a drizzle of your best olive oil.

Relax and Rejuvenate in the Sauna

Alaska is a wild land where many people live in remote areas. Many homes are "dry," meaning they don't have running water, showers, or indoor plumbing. It's popular in Alaska to use saunas—known also by the Yup'ik word *maqivik* or Russian word *banya*—to bathe and heal. For thousands of years, Alaska Natives have taken steam baths to treat ailments, purify the sick, prepare hunters for the chase, strengthen warriors for battle, and ready pregnant women for labor. Today in Alaskan culture, steam bathing is a favorite way to relax and rejuvenate both physically and mentally. It's a place for conversation, quiet, and community; a place to warm up and just be in your body. Try these sauna tips:

Fill up buckets with water and haul them into the sauna. Put a big pot or kettle of water on top of the stove to heat up once the sauna stove is lit and keep some water in a bucket on the floor so it stays cold and refreshing.

Light a candle in the sauna for dim light to see by.

Bring lots of water to drink. It's important to stay hydrated while you're hot and sweaty.

Sit up high for a more intense heat or on a lower level for gentler temperatures. As your body warms up, take advantage of some quiet time for breathing and stretching.

Use a ladle to throw a little water onto the hot stove and rocks to let the room steam up. Breathe deeply and let the steam bath purify your body and mind. Repeat this regularly during your sauna.

Add a few drops of invigorating essential oils, like eucalyptus or peppermint, to your steam bath and breathe in the aromatherapy.

Take breaks outside in the snow or do a cold plunge in the sea or cold water nearby. Repeat the hot-cold therapy to enliven your spirit and clear your mind.

Scrub down with body brushes, loofahs, pumice stones, salt scrubs, and soap once your skin has sweated and softened. Shampoo your hair and give yourself a final rise by mixing the hot water into the bucket of cold water until you find a desirable, refreshing temperature to scoop over your head or dunk your head into.

Sit outside in your towel and enjoy the stars or scenery, feel the aliveness in your body, and the clarity in your mind. Drink lots of water and get some rest.

Smoked Salmon Pesto Pizza

4 ounces goat cheese, softened
2 ounces cream cheese, softened
Zest of 1 medium lemon
Kosher salt and freshly ground pepper
1 portion homemade or store-bought pizza dough
Extra-virgin olive oil
1 cup basil pesto
½ cup fresh mozzarella, cut into 1-inch pieces
1 cup cherry tomato medley, cut in half
½ medium red onion, thinly sliced
3 tablespoons capers, drained
2 cups baby arugula
6 ounces smoked salmon, flaked apart
Fresh dill, chopped
Champagne or white wine vinegar

If we can, we find a way to add fish to any dish, and pizza is no exception. Making pizza at home is a fun and hands-on family meal that everyone can help prepare and enjoy. We let the pizza dough rise throughout the day while we're fishing, and after we anchor up for the night, everyone on the crew gets to decorate their own pie with ingredients they find on board. Some combinations are classic—smoked salmon and pesto is one of these.

Makes 1 large pizza

In a small bowl, mix together the goat cheese, cream cheese, lemon zest, and salt and pepper to taste.

Preheat the oven to 400 degrees F. Line a pizza pan with parchment paper.

Roll out the pizza dough and transfer to the prepared pan. Using a pastry brush or your finger, coat just the outer 1-inch border of the dough (what will be the raised edge) with olive oil.

Using a large spoon, spread the pesto evenly, avoiding the oiled edge of the dough.

Top the pie with the mozzarella pieces, then add dollops of the goat cheese mixture. Sprinkle the tomatoes, half the onion slices, and half the capers evenly across the pie, avoiding the edges.

Season lightly with salt and pepper.

Bake until the crust is golden brown and the cheese is melted and bubbly, 15 to 20 minutes.

While the pizza bakes, in a medium bowl, gently toss the arugula with the salmon, dill, and the remaining capers and onions. Add a splash of olive oil and vinegar and season lightly with salt and pepper. Garnish the pie with the arugula and salmon mixture and serve.

Go Ice Fishing

SUPPLIES LIST

- fishing license
- warm clothes and boots
- a fishing friend
- first-aid kit
- extra warm clothes and dry socks
- ice fishing pole and lure
- bait
- ice auger
- ice scoop
- camp chair or camping pad
- hot drinks or soup
- radio

There are many ways to bundle up and experience the outdoors in winter—but sometimes you'd rather sit on a comfy chair with a hot drink in hand instead of breaking out the skis. Ice fishing is a great way to spend time outside with friends and family of all ages without gearing up for an extreme adventure. Ice fishing is a fun and chill way to enjoy the winter landscape together while catching dinner. It's basically winter tailgating! Here are some tips to get started.

Purchase a fishing license that's valid in the state where you'll be fishing.

Check the fishing regulations that apply to your fishing location. Learn how to properly identify each different species that you catch.

Decide when and where to fish. Check the weather forecast, dress appropriately, wear ice cleats for traction, and educate yourself on fishing safety. Learn which frozen waterways in your area are both safe and likely to hold fish.

Bring a fishing friend (or, even better, a fishing mentor who can share their wisdom). It's safer to have someone who can assist if you find yourself in a dangerous position. Leave word with friends or family about when you're leaving and when you plan to be back. Be as specific as you can about your location. Bring a first-aid kit, extra warm clothes, and dry socks stored in a waterproof dry bag, so if you do go for a swim you can change immediately.

Use a fishing rod that has plenty of sensitivity but is shorter than a standard open-water rod. Most ice fishing rods are 3 to 4 feet in length. Use an ultralight spinning or spin-casting reel rigged with a heavy (8-pound) fishing line that won't snap in the cold.

Pick your bait (live or artificial). Live bait like minnows or wax worms can be better for beginners; once you have some experience, you can switch to jigs, spoons, or other artificial lures to make fishing more of a challenge.

Test the ice for safety. Look for hard, clear, and "blue" ice with no visible cracks. Avoid black, pitted, slushy ice that's spiderwebbed with frozen fissures. Ice is thickest closer to shore. As you travel farther away, use your auger to drill test holes and measure the ice thickness. Minimum ice measurements to keep you from taking a polar bear plunge: 4 inches of ice for walking safety, 5 to 7 inches of ice for an ATV or snow machine, 8 to 12 inches of ice for a vehicle. If you're unsure, contact your local fish and game office, or check with a local sporting goods store for conditions.

Drill a hole using an ice auger. Using extreme care, position the auger blades on the ice and apply pressure as you drill the hole. Don't forget to bring an ice scoop to remove ice buildup from your fishing hole.

Rig your lines using your bait or lure and allow the bait to fall to the bottom. Once the line hits the bottom, reel it up a foot or two. You're fishing! Just wait to feel a bite and reel in your catch.

Don't forget to get comfy! Bring a camp chair to sit in, a cup of hot cocoa, and a thermos of tasty soup. If you prefer, bring a camping pad to kneel on. Maybe your dog is curled up on a plush dog bed, maybe there's a portable radio playing, maybe you're posted up in a fish house next to a glowing red heater, maybe life is good.

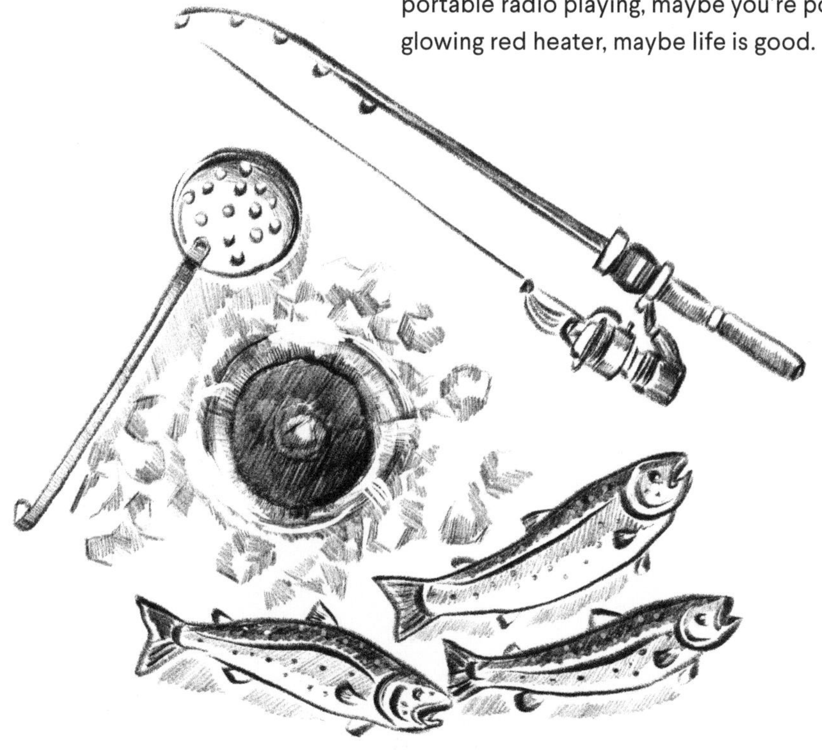

Fish Pie with Lemon-Dill Cream Sauce

- 3 tablespoons unsalted butter
- 1 red onion, diced
- 8 ounces mushrooms, cleaned and sliced
- ½ head green cabbage, cored and shredded
- 1 tablespoon red wine vinegar
- Kosher salt and freshly ground black pepper
- 1 tablespoon extra-virgin olive oil
- 1 skinless wild salmon fillet (about 1 pound)
- 2 sheets homemade or store-bought puff pastry
- 2 cups cooked short-grain brown rice
- 2 hard-boiled eggs
- ½ cup shredded sharp cheddar cheese
- ½ cup fine bread crumbs
- 2 tablespoons minced fresh dill
- ⅓ cup heavy cream
- 1 egg, beaten
- Lemon-Dill Cream Sauce (recipe follows)

Fish pie came to Alaska with Russian fur traders from across the Bering Strait in the eighteenth century. Long after Russians sold their claim of the territory to the United States, the dish remained a staple in Alaskan food culture. Fish pie, also known locally as *perok*, is a warming winter comfort food featuring a flaky buttery crust, salmon, rice, hard-boiled eggs, savory mushrooms, cheese, and cabbage. It's a great way to use up salmon from your freezer, as well as leftover rice and vegetables. This recipe is adapted from local Homer chef Kirsten Dixon's "Russian Salmon Pie" recipe, featured in *New York Times Cooking.*

Makes 1 (10-inch) pie

Preheat the oven to 375 degrees F.

Melt the butter in a large nonstick skillet over medium-low heat. Add the onion and cook until tender, stirring occasionally, about 7 minutes. Add the mushrooms, cabbage, and vinegar; increase the heat to medium. Cover the pan and cook for 7 minutes, stirring once or twice. Remove the vegetables from the pan, season with salt and pepper to taste, and set aside.

Wipe out the skillet, add the oil, and set to medium-high heat. Add the salmon and season lightly with salt and pepper. Cook the salmon 5 minutes per side; remove from the pan and let cool on a plate. Flake the salmon into large chunks and set aside.

Place a sheet of puff pastry on a lightly floured surface. Gently roll out the pastry until it is large enough to fit a 10-inch cast-iron pan. Transfer the pastry to the pan, allowing extra dough to drape over the edge.

Spread the brown rice over the bottom of the pastry. Peel and slice the hard-boiled eggs and add to the pie, followed by the flaked salmon. Sprinkle with the cheese, then bread crumbs. Arrange the vegetable mixture on top. Sprinkle with the dill and a drizzle of cream. ⟶

Roll out the remaining sheet of puff pastry on a lightly floured surface until it is large enough to cover the pie. Brush the rim of the bottom pastry with water and place the second sheet of pastry directly on top. Using scissors or a knife, trim off the excess dough. Use a fork to crimp the edges of the pie together to help the sheets of pastry adhere.

Cut a few small slits in the top of the pie to allow steam to escape. Brush the top of the pie with the beaten egg. Bake until the pastry is puffed and golden brown, 35 to 40 minutes. Cool for 10 minutes. Serve with a drizzle of the Lemon-Dill Cream Sauce.

LEMON-DILL CREAM SAUCE

½ cup mayonnaise
1½ tablespoons fresh dill
1 tablespoon whole milk
1 medium lemon, first zested, then juiced
Pinch of kosher salt

In a small bowl, combine the mayonnaise, dill, milk, 1 tablespoon lemon juice, 2 teaspoons lemon zest, and salt. Stir until well combined.

Make Winter Bird Garlands

SUPPLIES LIST

- Dried rose hips
- strong natural thread or twine
- a large strong needle
- dried orange slices
- dried apple rings
- stale popcorn
- cranberries
- raisins
- peanuts (in the shell)
- other fruits or nuts

Invite the birds over for a solstice snack! String up tasty treats outdoors—on the trees, in your garden, or outside your window—so you can enjoy watching the winged friends that stop by. Different species of birds like different treats; observe what your visitors like to eat! Check that all the feed you're using is safe for birds and wildlife to consume and keep your garland out of reach of pets. Once you have enjoyed the garland, put any leftovers in the compost bin and add the twine if it is compostable.

Cut a length of twine to the size you'd like for the garland. Tie a knot at one end.

Thread a large needle with the twine on the end opposite the knot. (If you're working with children, use a blunt safety needle.)

Push the needle through each ingredient and push it toward the knotted end of the twine. Try creating a pattern with the ingredients.

Once your garland is full of tasty treats, remove the needle and secure the end with a knot before hanging it.

Fancy Crab Mac & Cheese

FOR THE CRUMB TOPPING:

1 tablespoon unsalted butter, plus more for greasing
1 tablespoon extra-virgin olive oil
1 cup panko bread crumbs
¼ cup grated Parmesan cheese

FOR THE MACARONI AND SAUCE:

1 pound elbow macaroni
¼ cup unsalted butter
1 shallot, finely sliced
3 cloves garlic, minced
3 tablespoons all-purpose flour
1 tablespoon Old Bay seasoning
2 cups whole milk
⅓ cup heavy cream
1 teaspoon kosher salt
½ teaspoon freshly ground black pepper
4 cups sharp white cheddar cheese
¼ cup grated Parmesan cheese
8 ounces (1¼ cups) crabmeat, plus ⅓ cup extra for the topping
Fresh parsley, chopped, for garnish

When winter begs for a comforting meal, pull out your big cast-iron pan and make a fancy mac & cheese with crabmeat. We subsistence harvest king, tanner, and Dungeness crab in the summer season in Alaska, bust out our big crab cooker on the back deck of our boat, and have a crab-cracking party with our crew to remove the meat so we can bag it up and freeze it for easy meals through the seasons. This recipe is delicious with any type of crab and is truly a delight for everyone who loves creamy, cheesy, crabby, golden-brown comfort food.

Makes 6 servings

Preheat the oven to 375 degrees F. Lightly butter a cast-iron pan or casserole dish.

To make the topping, heat the butter and oil in a medium skillet over medium heat. Add the panko and cook, stirring, until lightly browned. Remove from the heat and stir in the Parmesan. Set aside.

To make the macaroni, cook the pasta in boiling salted water until al dente. Drain well.

Melt the butter in a medium saucepan over medium heat. Add the shallot and garlic and cook, stirring, until fragrant and softened, about 3 minutes. Add the flour and Old Bay seasoning and cook until golden brown, about 1 minute. Whisk in the milk and cream and cook, stirring constantly, until thickened and smooth. Stir in the salt and pepper. Remove from the heat and add the cheeses, stirring to melt. Gently fold in the 1¼ cups crabmeat and the cooked pasta.

Spoon the pasta mixture into the prepared pan. Arrange the extra crabmeat on top and sprinkle evenly with the bread-crumb topping and parsley. Bake until golden brown and bubbling, 25 to 30 minutes.

Shrimp and Crab Gumbo

½ cup (1 stick) unsalted butter, divided
6 tablespoons all-purpose flour
2 pounds okra, trimmed and chopped (thawed if frozen)
1 large yellow onion, diced
4 ribs celery, thinly sliced
1 large green bell pepper, diced
1 fennel bulb, cut into eight wedges
5 cloves garlic, minced
2 teaspoons dried oregano
2 teaspoons dried thyme
2 tablespoons gumbo filé powder
Kosher salt and freshly ground black pepper
Hot sauce, such as Crystal
2 quarts chicken or seafood stock
5 pounds large peeled wild shrimp, deveined and rinsed
1 pound crabmeat (such as Dungeness or king)
12 ounces smoked andouille sausage, cooked and sliced
6 cups cooked white rice
1 bunch flat-leaf parsley, leaves only, finely chopped
1 bunch green onions, both white and green parts, finely chopped

If you're familiar with Cajun cooking, you know there are a thousand ways to make a gumbo. Most families in Louisiana have their own generations-old gumbo tradition, including our in-laws and friends, who have inspired many Southern meals in our Northern kitchen. Louisiana and Alaska share a love for good seafood, and this recipe uses ingredients that could be sourced in an Alaskan grocery store and from local waters. Stock your pantry with filé powder—a thickener made from sassafras trees commonly used in soups and gumbos—so you can make this seafood dish a staple comfort food in your kitchen and turn it into a tradition of your own.

Makes 6 to 8 servings

In a large heavy pot, make a roux by melting 6 tablespoons of the butter over medium-high heat until browned. Stir in the flour and cook, stirring constantly, until golden brown, 8 to 10 minutes. Transfer the roux to a small bowl and set aside.

Add the remaining 2 tablespoons of butter to the same pot over medium-high heat. Add the okra, onion, celery, bell pepper, fennel, and garlic and cook for 10 minutes, until the vegetables have softened. Add the oregano, thyme, and filé powder, and the salt, black pepper, and hot sauce to taste. Cook for 2 minutes. Add the reserved roux and stir to combine. Whisk in the stock and simmer for 45 minutes. Add the shrimp, crabmeat, and sausage and continue to simmer for another 10 minutes, until shrimp are cooked through.

Let the gumbo rest for at least 20 minutes. To serve, reheat and ladle the gumbo over hot rice and garnish with the parsley and green onions.

Pour Homemade Candles

SUPPLIES LIST

All-natural beeswax or soy wax (blocks or flakes). To estimate how much wax you'll need, measure the volume of your vessels by filling each container with water, then pour the water into a measuring cup. For every 1 fluid ounce (in volume) your container holds, you'll need about 1 ounce (in weight) of wax.

Candle vessels (such as heat-proof jars, glasses, ceramic vessels, or tins). Look for unique containers at a local vintage store. Or reuse an old candle container: place it in simmering water to melt any remaining wax, then clean it with a paper towel.

Pre-waxed wicks with metal tabs on one end: for small candles use thin wicks; for large candles use thick wicks. Check that the wick will work with the type of wax you choose. Flat braided cotton is a good general-purpose wick.

There's nothing cozier than a home lit with the soft, warm light of glowing candles. We love starting our day around a candlelit table with a hot cup of coffee and friends. Candles in a tin are handy to take camping or on a winter cabin trip, and they make a delicious-smelling handcrafted gift. Candles can be expensive to buy, but it's easy and economical to make them at home. A batch only takes an hour or so, the supplies are relatively few and inexpensive, and cleanup is a breeze.

Fill a large pot halfway with water and bring it to a simmer on the stovetop. Put the wax in a smaller pot or saucepan and lower it into the simmering water, being careful to avoid splashing any water into the wax. Allow the wax to melt, stirring occasionally. When the wax is fully melted it will register about 180 degrees F on a thermometer and have the thickness of olive oil. Remove the melting pot from the heat and let the wax cool to between 120 degrees F and 140 degrees F before adding fragrance or pouring the candles.

While waiting for the wax to cool, prepare the candle containers. Place a little superglue or hot glue on the metal bottom of a wick and press it to the bottom center of the container. If using large containers, you may want to use multiple wicks spaced evenly.

Stabilize the wick by snipping a small hole in the middle of a piece of masking tape a few inches longer than the rim of the container. Guide the top of the wick through the hole. Attach the ends of the tape on each side of the container's rim to hold the wick upright for pouring.

Once the wax has cooled to the proper temperature, stir in the fragrance, if desired.

- Superglue or hot glue
- Melting pot or old saucepan
- Large pot, to use as a double boiler
- Mixing spoon
- Candy thermometer
- Masking tape
- Paper towels
- Fragrance (optional): Beeswax has a beautiful natural scent, but if you'd like to add fragrance to your candle, use natural essential oils or fragrance oils intended for candle-making, as some oils are flammable. Add 1 ounce fragrance per 1 pound wax.

Pour the wax from the pot into the containers slowly and carefully to avoid the tape and wick and to keep from creating air bubbles. Let the candles cool and harden at room temperature for at least 24 hours. Remove the tape and trim the wick to ¼ inch.

Start the cleanup while the wax is still liquid. Use a paper towel to wipe remaining wax from the spoon, thermometer, and inside of the melting pot, then wash the equipment with soap and water.

Salted Caramel Apple Pie

FOR THE CRUST:

- 2½ cups all-purpose flour
- 2 teaspoons granulated sugar
- 1 teaspoon kosher salt
- 1 cup (2 sticks) cold unsalted butter, cut into ½-inch pieces
- 1 cup cold water
- ¼ cup apple cider vinegar

FOR THE CARAMEL:

- 1 cup plus 2 tablespoons granulated sugar
- ¼ cup water
- ½ cup (1 stick) unsalted butter
- ½ cup heavy cream
- 1 teaspoon kosher salt

FOR THE FILLING:

- 2 medium lemons
- 6 to 7 baking apples (about 2½ pounds), peeled, cored, and thinly sliced
- ⅓ cup light brown sugar
- 2 tablespoons all-purpose flour
- ¼ teaspoon ground cinnamon
- ¼ teaspoon ground allspice
- ¼ teaspoon freshly grated nutmeg
- ¼ teaspoon kosher salt
- Pinch of freshly ground black pepper
- 2 to 3 dashes Angostura bitters (or orange bitters)

A flaky, buttery crust, soft spiced apples, and a salted caramel drizzle make this pie one of our favorite winter desserts and a twist on an old classic. Baking in winter is a lovely way to fill your house with warmth and flavor, and apples are one of the few fruits we can count on our small town's grocery store to stock through the seasons. That makes apple pies common in Alaska—and we can't complain. Enjoy leftovers for breakfast with a cup of coffee or tea.

Makes 1 double-crust 9-inch pie

To make the crust, in a large bowl, combine the flour, sugar and salt. Add the butter pieces and coat with the flour mixture using a spatula. With a pastry cutter, cut the butter into the flour mixture, working quickly, until mostly pea-size pieces of butter remain. (A few larger pieces are okay; do not overblend.)

In a large measuring cup or small bowl, combine the water, apple cider vinegar, and 1 cup of ice. Sprinkle the ice water over the flour mixture 1 tablespoon at a time, mixing the dough with a scraper or spatula until it is fully incorporated and the dough just comes together. It should be moist, but not wet. Shape the dough into two equal-size flat discs, wrap in plastic, and refrigerate for at least 1 hour or overnight.

To make the salted caramel, in a medium saucepan over low heat, add the sugar and water and stir until just dissolved. Add the butter and bring to a low boil. Continue cooking at a low boil until the mixture turns golden brown, 8 to 12 minutes. Remove the mixture from the heat and immediately add the heavy cream. It will bubble and steam. Whisk in the salt. Set the caramel aside while you prepare the apple filling.

To make the apple filling, juice the lemons into a large bowl. Dredge all the apple slices in the lemon juice to prevent browning and add flavor. Set aside.

In a small bowl, combine the sugar, flour, cinnamon, allspice, nutmeg, salt, pepper, and bitters. Sprinkle this mixture over the apples in the bowl, using your hands to gently mix and coat the apple slices.

Preheat the oven to 375 degrees F.

FOR FINISHING:
Egg wash (1 large egg whisked with 1 teaspoon water and a pinch of kosher salt) (optional)
Demerara or other large-grain sugar, for finishing
Cinnamon, for finishing
¼ teaspoon flaky sea salt

To roll out the pastry, place one disc of the chilled dough on a lightly floured surface. Using a floured rolling pin, roll out the dough into a 12-inch circle. Transfer the dough to the pie pan, leaving a 1-inch overhang.

Layer one-third of the apples in the bottom of the crust so that there are minimal gaps. Pour one-third of the caramel over the apples. Add another one-third each of the apples and caramel for a second layer, then add a third layer from the remaining apples and caramel; save a small portion of caramel to pour on top once the pie is assembled.

Make a lattice top crust by rolling out the second disc of dough into a 12-inch circle and cutting the dough into 1-inch-thick strips. Place half the dough strips parallel to each other across the top of the filled pie. The longest strips should be in the center of the pie. Weave the remaining strips over and under each of the parallel strips to create a lattice or checkerboard pattern. Gently pinch together the lattice strip edges and the overhanging dough of the bottom crust; crimp the edges to seal the top and bottom crusts together.

To finish the crust, brush the lattice all over with a milk or egg wash to encourage browning. Sprinkle the top with sugar and cinnamon. Drizzle with the reserved caramel and sprinkle with flaky sea salt.

Set a rimmed baking sheet on a lower rack in the oven to contain any overflow while baking. Bake the pie at 375 degrees F for 20 minutes. Reduce the oven temperature to 325 degrees F and bake for an additional 30 minutes. Test the apples for doneness with a long skewer or small knife. The apples should be just soft. Let the pie cool, then slice and enjoy!

WINTER SOLSTICE FEAST

MENU

Rosemary Negroni
page 222

Roasted Broccolini and Carrots with Tahini Dressing
page 225

Oyster Stew
page 226

Salmon Dumplings
page 229

Chewy Ginger Chocolate Cookies
page 231

Set the table with many candles, colorful dishes, rosemary, eucalyptus, or dried flowers. Make use of extra hands and have a dumpling-making party with your guests. Fill small bowls with steaming buttery oyster stew to enjoy while you roast broccolini and carrots smothered in tahini for the table. Set out chopsticks and small dishes of soy sauce for casual dumpling dining. Negronis with infused rosemary and gooey, chewy ginger chocolate cookies make the perfect bookmark to the night around the crackling bonfire or woodstove.

Rosemary Negroni

FOR THE INFUSED GIN:

3 (10-inch) sprigs rosemary
1 (750-ml) bottle of gin

FOR THE NEGRONI COCKTAIL:

1 orange slice
1 ounce Campari
1 ounce vermouth
1 ounce rosemary-infused gin

A spirit-forward classic cocktail made with homemade rosemary-infused gin. You'll need only a few simple ingredients. Then put your feet up and sip in front of the fire or while enjoying a card game or a good book. We keep ingredients for this cocktail on hand throughout the holidays to bring merriment wherever we go. Its bright-red color is a cheerful addition to any table.

Makes 1 negroni

To make the infused gin, rub the rosemary between your hands to release its aromas. Place the sprigs in the bottle of gin, cap the bottle, and swirl a few times. Infuse the gin for 4 days at room temperature. Strain the gin and discard the rosemary.

To make the negroni, squeeze juice from the orange wedge into a cocktail shaker and then set the orange wedge in a chilled cocktail glass. Add liquors to the shaker and shake vigorously. Strain into a chilled glass. Finish with a sprig of rosemary. Enjoy.

STORIES FROM ALASKAN WOMEN ON CELEBRATING WINTER

"Cross-country skiing daily if the weather cooperates, eating well, embracing the slower days, and giving myself permission to do less, as in recovering from the overdrive days of summer light."

—LINDA VAN HOUTEN, FAIRBANKS, ALASKA (TANANA LAND)

"I keep the candles and the fire lit and make lots of comfort food: sourdough bread and cinnamon rolls, cabbage dishes, and our favorite: moose pot pie. We mix home-canned crab-apple juice with ginger ale to enjoy with dinner. And pull rhubarb from the freezer for pies and muffins, and maybe a batch of jam. We put local honey purchased from our neighbor on everything. On Fridays in the winter, I make homemade pizza on pizza stones so we can stay home and watch a movie together. Even the first power outage is celebrated, with candles and kerosene lanterns and popcorn popped in Dutch ovens on the stove."

—KATE ROBINSON, FAIRBANKS, ALASKA (TANANA LAND)

Roasted Broccolini and Carrots with Tahini Dressing

FOR THE SAUCE:
¼ cup tahini
3 tablespoons water
1 tablespoon freshly squeezed lemon juice
2 teaspoons honey
1 clove garlic, pressed or grated
¼ teaspoon kosher salt
¼ teaspoon freshly ground black pepper

FOR THE VEGETABLES:
8 ounces broccolini, ends trimmed
8 ounces carrots (cut larger carrots in half lengthwise)
1 tablespoon extra-virgin olive oil
¼ teaspoon kosher salt
¼ teaspoon freshly ground black pepper
1 clove garlic, minced

FOR THE GARNISH:
¼ cup toasted flaked almonds, pine nuts, or pumpkin seeds

These roasted vegetables make a delicious side dish to seafood or addition to a grain bowl or flatbread. Broccolini (and broccoli) and carrots are standard vegetables year-round in Alaska, and it's nice to spruce them up with something special, like creamy tahini dressing and toasted nuts. Roasting vegetables is easy and, tossed with a simple seasoning, so flavorful.

Makes about 4 servings

Preheat the oven to 425 degrees F.

To make the sauce, in a glass jar or small bowl combine the tahini, water, lemon juice, honey, garlic, salt, and pepper and mix well. Set aside to allow the flavors to blend while the vegetables roast.

To make the vegetables, on a baking sheet, toss the broccolini and carrots with the oil and sprinkle with the salt, pepper, and garlic.

Roast the vegetables until the broccolini trees are slightly browned and crunchy and the carrots are tender, 12 to 15 minutes.

Transfer the vegetables to a serving platter. Allow to cool until warm, then drizzle with the tahini sauce and sprinkle with the nuts. Serve warm or at room temperature.

Oyster Stew

- ¼ cup unsalted butter
- 1 large yellow onion, finely diced
- 2 cloves garlic, grated or minced
- ½ teaspoon freshly ground black pepper
- ¼ teaspoon cayenne
- ¼ teaspoon paprika
- ¼ teaspoon kosher salt
- 6 cups whole milk or half-and-half
- 1 teaspoon dried parsley
- 1 pound fresh raw oysters, shucked, oyster liquor reserved

We are lucky to live where oysters thrive in the clean saltwater of Alaska's coastline. Oysters harvested from the coves and inlets of Kachemak Bay are sweet and plump, perfectly shucked and slurped on the spot. In winter, though, when we're craving something warm and comforting, we love oysters in this creamy stew, inspired by M. F. K. Fisher's recipe from a book that's a staple on our bookshelf: *Consider the Oyster*. Its ingredients are simple, its broth is luxurious, and you can taste the richness of the ocean with each spoonful.

Makes about 4 servings

Melt the butter in a heavy-bottom saucepan over medium heat. Add the onion and cook until tender, about 5 minutes. Add the garlic and cook for another 1 to 2 minutes, taking care to not burn the garlic. Stir in the black pepper, cayenne, paprika, and salt, and cook for about 1 minute. Reduce the heat to low and add the milk, parsley, and oyster liquor.

Continue cooking over low heat until the mixture is hot, begins to steam, and bubbles just start to appear around the edges. Do not allow it to come to a boil. Remove from the heat and season to taste with salt and pepper.

Add the oysters and cook over low heat until the oysters begin to curl up on the edges. Ladle into the bowls and enjoy immediately.

Salmon Dumplings

FOR THE DUMPLINGS:
1 fillet (about 1 pound) wild Alaska salmon, skinned and deboned
4 green onions, both white and green parts, chopped
2 cloves garlic, diced
1 tablespoon grated fresh ginger
1 tablespoon fish sauce
1 tablespoon soy sauce
½ teaspoon sesame oil
½ teaspoon rice wine vinegar
¼ teaspoon red pepper flakes
20 gyoza wrappers
Extra-virgin olive oil, for frying

FOR THE DIPPING SAUCE:
2 tablespoons soy sauce
2 tablespoons unseasoned rice vinegar
1 tablespoon dark brown sugar
1 teaspoon sesame oil
¼ teaspoon red pepper flakes

Salmon dumplings are a fun food to make with many hands. Invite family and friends over to help assemble these chewy, golden, crispy dumplings filled with salmon, ginger, and alliums. We use fish thawed from our freezer, but you're welcome to use fresh fish if you're making this recipe during salmon season. These dumplings are best with an hour in the freezer after forming, just enough time to have a leisurely cocktail in front of the fire before you cook.

Makes 20 dumplings

To make the dumplings, finely chop the salmon (or pulse in a food processor) and place in a large bowl. Add the green onions, garlic, and ginger and mix well. Stir in the fish sauce, soy sauce, sesame oil, vinegar, and red pepper flakes and mix until evenly combined. Place the mixture in the refrigerator to cool for at least 30 minutes.

Line a baking sheet with waxed or parchment paper.

Place a heaping tablespoon of the salmon mix in the middle of a wrapper. Using a bowl of water to keep your fingertips moistened, fold the wrapper in half and slowly pinch the edges diagonally together. The water will help the edges of the wrapper adhere.

Place filled dumplings on the waxed paper, keeping them spaced apart. When finished, transfer the baking sheet to the freezer. Freeze for at least 1 hour.

To make the dipping sauce, in a small bowl, combine the soy sauce, vinegar, brown sugar, sesame oil, and red pepper flakes.

When you're ready to cook the dumplings, heat a small amount of olive oil in a large skillet with a lid over medium-high heat. Place the dumplings in the skillet and cook until the bottoms brown slightly, 2 to 3 minutes. Pour ½ cup of water into the skillet and cover with a lid to trap the steam.

Reduce the heat to medium and allow the dumplings to steam until the wrappers become slightly opaque, about 9 minutes. Remove from the pan and arrange on a serving plate. Enjoy the dumplings with chopsticks, dipped in sauce.

Chewy Ginger Chocolate Cookies

- 1 cup (2 sticks) unsalted butter, softened
- 1 cup dark brown sugar
- 1 cup light molasses
- 2 tablespoons grated fresh ginger
- 3 cups plus 2 tablespoons all-purpose flour
- 2 tablespoons cocoa powder
- 3 teaspoons ground ginger
- 2 teaspoons ground cinnamon
- ½ teaspoon ground cloves
- ½ teaspoon freshly grated nutmeg
- 2 teaspoons baking soda
- 1 tablespoon boiling water
- 12 ounces semisweet chocolate chips
- 1 cup granulated sugar, for coating

During the holidays growing up, we would bundle up and head to our small town's beloved bakery by the sea for chocolatey, gingerbready cookies and walk down to the snowy beach to eat them. This recipe is inspired by those, and they are treats we enjoy baking around the holidays, dropping batches off with our local postal carriers and leaving on friends' doorsteps. We especially love the fresh flavor the grated ginger adds to these soft, chewy cookies.

Makes about 28 cookies

In a large bowl, with a handheld mixer, cream the butter, brown sugar, molasses, and ginger until light and fluffy, 2 to 3 minutes.

In a medium bowl, sift together the flour, cocoa powder, and spices. Add half of this mixture to the butter mixture. Stir to combine.

In a small bowl, dissolve the baking soda in the boiling water. Add the liquid and the remaining flour mixture into the butter mixture and stir well to combine. Fold in the chocolate chips.

Chill the dough in the refrigerator for at least 20 minutes. Place the granulated sugar in a bowl.

While the dough chills, preheat the oven to 325 degrees F. Line a baking sheet with parchment paper.

Roll the dough into 1-inch balls and then toss them in the granulated sugar to coat. Place dough balls on the baking sheet with several inches of space in between them to allow the cookies to expand while baking. Bake for 10 to 12 minutes, until still soft in the center and slightly crisped on the edges. If you make larger cookies, flatten them slightly before baking. Let the cookies cool on a wire rack.

STORIES FROM ALASKAN WOMEN ON THRIVING IN WINTER

"To live in Alaska year-round, you should embrace the cycle, instead of fighting it. The midnight sun spurs us on all summer, energizing us for all the work to be done. The decaying winter sun lulls us to sleep, and I try to flow with it. The kid and I cuddle around the woodstove, reading aloud, and after school is done we have tea in the late afternoon as the sunlight wanes. The sun coming back in February tells us it's time to get outside again! We go to the ice park, the start of the dog races, take the snow machines out, go ice fishing, and start listening for the sound of trickling water."

—KATE ROBINSON, FAIRBANKS, ALASKA (TANANA LAND)

"Give yourself permission to slow down. I'm a transplant and always prided myself on being a 'get 'er done' highly productive person when working as a grad student and training for ultramarathons. The time to get it done is fishing season and we rise to the occasion. In the winter, it's okay to bake cookies and binge-watch *Buffy the Vampire Slayer*. Random acts of kindness also have helped—both doing them and being the recipient of them. It's a way to say to the community 'I'm here for you' even while we cozy up indoors."

—LIBERTY SIEGLE, SITKA, ALASKA (TLINGIT LAND)

"I've spent thirty-five winters in Alaska, and my best advice for thriving in winter is to go outside. It will be cold. You might not like it at first. But if you gear up and dress warmly, you can enjoy the biggest outdoor playground in the world. Skiing, skating, snowshoeing, snowboarding, fat biking, skijoring—find what you're into and go do it!"

—KYLIE EADS, FAIRBANKS, ALASKA (TANANA LAND)

"My best advice is to make peace with the snow, or at a minimum, don't hate it. Love or hate it, either way, you'll still have the same amount of snow and you may as well not be miserable. Too many people move to Southeast Alaska and complain about the rain. You can't live in Fairbanks and be surprised when the dark comes—you have to make your own light and move through the seasons fluidly. We cannot fight Mother Nature and must find a way to be at peace through the sleepy time of year."

—HEATHER DARCE, HOMER, ALASKA (DENA'INA LAND)

"Get outside with your people. Potluck, prepare food together, hunt food together, cook on a fire, ice skate on a glacial lake, snowshoe the same trails you hike the rest of the year, and suck in the solitude."

—JANEL HARRIS, SELDOVIA, ALASKA (ALUTIIQ, UNANGAX̂, DENA'INA LAND)

A Final Note

We hope the pages of this book inspire you to get fresh air in any weather, gather with friends and family to cook and share good food together, feel the delights of the changing seasons and celebrate your harvest. We grew up in Alaska and have been molded and moved by the land, water, and people here. It is a wild place that asks for capability and reverence, and has challenged us to be self-sufficient in many ways, but also taught us to lean into our community through those challenges. This place has guided us to a deep connection with the natural world and a life lived by the rhythms of the seasons. It's a good life and we're grateful to be able to share it with you.

We invite you to join us in a lifelong quest of knowing the land and its gifts, and giving back in return. When fishing or picking berries, it is important to be respectful. Take only what you need and leave some behind for other people and creatures who share the oceans and forest. Use everything you gather or catch, do not waste it. Learn about the history of the land you inhabit and harvest from; find out whose traditional territory it is, its Indigenous name, and who the Native people are who still live there today. Learn about the human impact that affects the wild places you depend on and love, and use your voice to help protect them, whether you make art, write to your legislators, vote, protest, volunteer, or get involved in other ways. Engage with the land; it is so alive, it teaches us so much if we listen.

No matter where you are reading this book, we hope the salty smell of the sea, the morning light on the mountains, and the lush taste of ripe blueberries and fresh salmon reach you. There's so much to celebrate every day we're alive. Thank you for being a part of our community and sharing in those gifts with us.

GRUNDÉNS

Acknowledgments

To the Alaska Natives, who have stewarded the land for generations.

To fishermen, fish processors, and all the people working to provide healthy wild seafood for people to eat.

To the harvesters, scientists, policy-makers, and stakeholders engaged in ensuring that Alaska's fisheries remain sustainable for generations to come.

To the Alaskan women's voices who contributed to these pages.

To our small team, who gracefully and passionately handles any new challenge, inspires us daily, and keeps everything shipshape when we head out fishing. We're honored to grow and learn alongside you. Thank you for helping us test these recipes!

To our mom and dad, who are the reason why we have a special story to tell and recipes to share. Thank you for raising us in the wild and for always putting family and good food first. And to Jacob and Peter, who are everything that's good and real—we love you.

Thanks to all the people of the Aleutian Islands who shared knowledge with our family about how to harvest and eat from the ocean and land when we began our life there.

Thank you, Dawn Heumann, who took the photographs for this book, for always being up for an Alaskan adventure. Your friendship is so special to us, and your talent as a professional creator is unmatched. We are honored to have worked on this project and eaten fish together in so many beautiful and remote corners of the state.

To Brian Grobleski, who artfully prepared these dishes to photograph. We've learned so much from the way you cook. Thank you for feeding us so well along the way!

Thank you to our editor, Jen Worick, an easygoing and enthusiastic collaborator throughout this wild process of making a book. Thank you for believing we'd get it done, giving us creative freedom, and listening to our dreams.

To the talented team at Sasquatch Books, it has been a delight to work with you again. Thank you, Anna Goldstein, for designing beautiful books.

To our agent, Sandra Bishop, thank you for your early and ongoing encouragement.

Thanks to Bunnell Street Arts Center and the many talented makers in Homer, Alaska, for lending us gorgeous dishes for our photo shoots.

Thank you, Christina Marie, for your stories and council on all good and hard things.

Finally, a sincere thanks to the community that has supported our small business since we started making T-shirts, and to the new friends and partners we've made along the way. Creating with you and for you has been our greatest joy.

Index

Note: Page numbers in *italic* refer to photographs.

A

Alaskan seasons, xvii–xix
Alaskan women, stories from, 20, 28, 63, 86, 92, 119, 154, 173, 180, 188, 222, 232
Anchovy Butter, Lemon-, 18
Anchovy-Herb Butter, 98
Apple, Rhubarb, and Cranberry Chutney, 144
Apple Pie, Salted Caramel, 218–219
Applesauce, Maple, 194
Avocado-Cilantro Crema, 153, *155*

B

Beets and Carrots with Anchovy-Herb Butter, Roasted, 98
berries
  Lemon Olive Oil Cake with Lemony Buttercream Frosting and Blueberries, *128*, 129
  Pick Wild Berries, *72*, 73
  Super Berry Muffins, 74, *75*
Birch Tree, Tap a, 42
Bird Garlands, Make Winter, 211
Biscuits, Smoked Salmon-Chive Buttermilk, 138
Black Cod with Wild Mushrooms and Kale over Creamy Grits, *178*, 179–180
breads
  Smoked Salmon-Chive Buttermilk Biscuits, 138
  Sourdough Cinnamon Rolls, *4*, 5–6
  Spring Greens and Sea Salt Sourdough Focaccia, *54*, 55–56
  Super Berry Muffins, 74, *75*
Broccolini and Carrots with Tahini Dressing, Roasted, *224*, 225
Bulbs Indoors, Grow, 189
Burgers with Wild Chimichurri, Halibut, *32*, 33–34
Butter, Anchovy-Herb, 98
Butters, Fancy Spring, 17–18

C

cake. *See* desserts
Candles, Pour Homemade, 216–217
Canning, Learn the Basics of, 140–143
Caper-Dill Cream, *8*, 9
Carrots with Anchovy-Herb Butter, Roasted Beets and, 98
Carrots with Tahini Dressing, Roasted Broccolini and, *224*, 225
caviar
  Crispy Smashed Potatoes with Salmon Caviar, 196, *197*
  Fancy Toast with Homemade Ricotta and Salmon Caviar, *84*, 85–86, *87*
  Make Salmon Caviar, 80–81
Charcuterie Board, Seafood, *174*, 175
Chimichurri Sauce, Wild, 34
Chocolate Peanut Butter Pie, 165
Chutney, Apple, Rhubarb, and Cranberry, 144
clams
  Alaska Seafood Boil; and variations, 125, *126–127*
  Dig for Clams, 36
  Lemony Clam Pasta with Crushed Pistachios, 37
cocktails. *See* drinks
Community, Share Your Harvest with Your, 107
Cook Fish over a Fire, *102*, 103
Cookies, Chewy Ginger Chocolate, *230*, 231
crab
  Alaska Seafood Boil; and variations, 125, *126–127*
  Crab Omelet with Wild Mushrooms, Caramelized Onion, and Brie, *136*, 137
  Fancy Crab Mac & Cheese, 212
  Shrimp and Crab Gumbo, *214*, 215
Curry with Chili Crisp, Sockeye Salmon Thai Red, *158*, 159

D

desserts
  Chewy Ginger Chocolate Cookies, *230*, 231
  Chocolate Peanut Butter Pie, 165
  Lemon Olive Oil Cake with Lemony Buttercream Frosting and Blueberries, *128*, 129
  Orange and Rosemary Upside-Down Cake, *182*, 183

Rhubarb-Cream–Filled Doughnuts, 43–44, *45*
Salted Caramel Apple Pie, 218–219
Sea Salt Fireweed-Honey Pie, 117
Spruce-Tip Ice Cream, *66*, 67
Dipping Sauce, *228*, 229
Doughnuts, Rhubarb-Cream–Filled, 43–44, *45*
drinks
Fireweed (Hard) Lemonade, 124
Fireweed Ice Cubes, 124
Fireweed Simple Syrup, 124
Fireweed-Infused Vodka, 124
Harvest Moon Old Fashioned, 173
Make Your Own Herbal Tea, 167
Nutty Cinnamon Banana Smoothie, 188
Rhubarb-Mint Gin & Tonic, 63
Rosemary Negroni, 222, *223*
Dumplings, Salmon, *228*, 229

E

eggs
Cast-Iron Baked Eggs, 77
Crab Omelet with Wild Mushrooms, Caramelized Onion, and Brie, *136*, 137
Smoked Salmon Scramble with Caper-Dill Cream on Toast, *8*, 9
Smoked Salmon Strata with Goat Cheese and Dill, 190, *191*

F

Fall Equinox Feast, *168*, 169–183, *170–171*
fiddleheads
Forage Fiddleheads, *22*, 23
Sautéed Fiddleheads with Pine Nuts, Lemon, and Oregano, 24, *25*
Fire, Cook Fish over a, *102*, 103
Fireweed (Hard) Lemonade, 124
Fireweed Ice Cubes, 124
Fireweed Simple Syrup, 124
Fireweed-Honey Pie, Sea Salt, 117
Fireweed-Infused Vodka, 124
fish. *See* black cod; halibut; salmon
Fish Pie with Lemon-Dill Cream Sauce, *206*, 207–208, *209*
fish/fishing traditions
Celebrate the First Fish, 79
Cook Fish over a Fire, *102*, 103
Go Ice Fishing, 204–205
Jig for a Halibut, *30*, 31
Make Fish Jerky, 94
Make Fish Stock, *114*, 115
Make Salmon Caviar, 80–81
Preserve Your Catch, 156–157
Share Your Harvest with Your Community, 107
Flower Bulbs Indoors, Grow, 189
flowers, edible
Eat Wildflowers, 116
Fireweed (Hard) Lemonade, 124
Fireweed Ice Cubes, 124
Fireweed Simple Syrup, 124
Fireweed-Infused Vodka, 124
Gather Rose Hips, 162, *163*
Spring Greens and Flower Salad, *52*, 53
Flowers, Press, 113
Focaccia, Spring Greens and Sea Salt Sourdough, *54*, 55–56
foraged ingredients
See also flowers, edible; mushrooms; seaweed
Forage Fiddleheads, *22*, 23
Forage Spruce Tips, 64, *65*
Harvest Wild Nettles, 26
Pick Wild Berries, *72*, 73
Sautéed Fiddleheads with Pine Nuts, Lemon, and Oregano, 24, *25*
Spring Greens and Flower Salad, *52*, 53
Spring Greens and Sea Salt Sourdough Focaccia, *54*, 55–56
Spruce-Tip Ice Cream, *66*, 67
Wild Chimichurri Sauce, 34
Wild Nettle Gnocchi, 27–28
Freeze Fish, 156–157
Furikake, 161

G

Garden, Harvest Seaweed for Your, 10–11
Garden, Plant an Herb, 16
Garden Italian Seasoning Blend, 161
Garden Vegetables, Quick Pickle Your, 148–149
Garlic Lemon Butter, 17
Gin & Tonic, Rhubarb-Mint, 63
Glaze, Honey-Cider, 147
Gnocchi, Wild Nettle, 27–28
Goat Cheese, Whipped, 196, *197*
Grits, Creamy, *178*, 179
Gumbo, Shrimp and Crab, *214*, 215

H

halibut
Grilled Halibut Tacos with Avocado-Cilantro Crema and Pickled Onions, 153–154, *155*
Halibut Burgers with Wild Chimichurri, *32*, 33–34
Jig for a Halibut, *30*, 31
Seafood Charcuterie Board, *174*, 175
herbs
Anchovy-Herb Butter, 98

Create Your Own Seasoning Blends, 161
Harvest & Dry Herbs, 152
Make Your Own Herbal Tea, 167
Plant an Herb Garden, 16
Honey-Cider Glaze, 147

I

Ice Cream, Spruce-Tip, *66*, 67
Ice Cubes, Fireweed, 124
Ice Fishing, Go, 204–205
Ice Lanterns, Light Up the Night with, 195
ingredients, pantry. *See* Pantry with Staples, Stock Your

J

Jar Fish, 157
Jerky, Make Fish, 94

K

kelp. *See* seaweed

L

Lanterns, Ice, Light Up the Night with, 195
Lemon Olive Oil Cake with Lemony Buttercream Frosting and Blueberries, *128*, 129
Lemon Rosemary Sea Salt, 161
Lemonade, Fireweed (Hard), 124
Lemon-Anchovy Butter, 18
Lemon-Dill Cream Sauce, Fish Pie with, *206*, 207–208, *209*
Lemony Clam Pasta with Crushed Pistachios, 37
Lemony Cream Dressing, 91
Lime-Cilantro Dressing, *96*, 97

M

Mac & Cheese, Fancy Crab, 212
Miso Salmon and Soba Salad Bowl, *110*, 111–112
Miso Seaweed Butter, 18
Muffins, Super Berry, 74, *75*
mushrooms
Black Cod with Wild Mushrooms and Kale over Creamy Grits, *178*, 179–180
Crab Omelet with Wild Mushrooms, Caramelized Onion, and Brie, *136*, 137
Fish Pie with Lemon-Dill Cream Sauce, *206*, 207–208, *209*
Forage Wild Mushrooms, 134–135
Miso Salmon and Soba Salad Bowl, *110*, 111–112
Sockeye Salmon Thai Red Curry with Chili Crisp, *158*, 159
Mussels with Spring Onions, Sorrel, Cider, and Cream, *58*, 59

N

Negroni, Rosemary, 222, *223*
nettles
Harvest Wild Nettles, 26
Wild Nettle Gnocchi, 27–28
Niçoise Sandwich, Tinned Salmon, 100, *101*
noodles. *See* pasta

O

Oats with Maple Applesauce and Walnuts, Creamy Steel-Cut, 194
Octopus, Avocado, and Tomato Salad with Lime-Cilantro Dressing, Tinned, *96*, 97
Old Fashioned, Harvest Moon, 173
Onions, Pickled, 153, *155*
Orange and Rosemary Upside-Down Cake, *182*, 183
oysters
Fried Oyster Toast, 99
Grilled Oysters with Miso Seaweed Butter, *46*, 47
Oyster Stew, 226
Seafood Charcuterie Board, *174*, 175

P

Pancakes, Pumpkin Spice, 139
Pantry with Staples, Stock Your, 192–193
Panzanella Salad, Smoked Salmon, *122*, 123
pasta
Fancy Crab Mac & Cheese, 212
Garlic-Butter Wild Alaska Spot Prawns with Stir-Fried Noodles, 164
Lemony Clam Pasta with Crushed Pistachios, 37
Miso Salmon and Soba Salad Bowl, *110*, 111–112
Tinned Salmon Carbonara with Arugula and Pine Nuts, *150*, 151
Wild Salmon Noodle Soup, *38*, 39–40
pickles
Dill Bullwhip Kelp Pickles, *14*, 15
Pickled Onions, 153, *155*
Quick Pickle Your Garden Vegetables, 148–149
Seafood Charcuterie Board, *174*, 175
Pie with Lemon-Dill Cream Sauce, Fish, *206*, 207–208, *209*
pies, dessert. *See* desserts
Pizza, Smoked Salmon Pesto, 200, *201*

Potato Gnocchi, Wild Nettle, 27–28
Potatoes with Salmon Caviar, Crispy Smashed, 196, *197*
prawns. *See* shrimp and prawns

R

rhubarb
Apple, Rhubarb, and Cranberry Chutney, 144
Rhubarb-Cream–Filled Doughnuts, 43–44, *45*
Rhubarb-Mint Gin & Tonic, 63
Rice with Toasted Almonds and Herbs, Crispy Turmeric, 146
Ricotta and Salmon Caviar, Fancy Toast with Homemade, *84*, 85–86, *87*
Rolls, Sourdough Cinnamon, *4*, 5–6
Rose Hips, Gather, 162, *163*

S

salads
Cured Salmon with Cucumber and Seaweed Salad in Lemony Cream Dressing, *90*, 91–92
Miso Salmon and Soba Salad Bowl, *110*, 111–112
Smoked Salmon Panzanella Salad, *122*, 123
Spring Greens and Flower Salad, *52*, 53
Tinned Octopus, Avocado, and Tomato Salad with Lime-Cilantro Dressing, *96*, 97
salmon
See also fish/fishing traditions
Crispy Smashed Potatoes with Salmon Caviar, 196, *197*
Cured Salmon with Cucumber and Seaweed Salad in Lemony Cream Dressing, *90*, 91–92
Fancy Toast with Homemade Ricotta and Salmon Caviar, *84*, 85–86, *87*
Fish Pie with Lemon-Dill Cream Sauce, *206*, 207–208, *209*
Make Salmon Caviar, 80–81
Miso Salmon and Soba Salad Bowl, *110*, 111–112
Salmon Dumplings, *228*, 229
Seafood Charcuterie Board, *174*, 175
Smoked Salmon Panzanella Salad, *122*, 123
Smoked Salmon Pesto Pizza, 200, *201*
Smoked Salmon Scramble with Caper-Dill Cream on Toast, *8*, 9
Smoked Salmon Strata with Goat Cheese and Dill, 190, *191*
Smoked Salmon-Chive Buttermilk Biscuits, 138
Smoky Citrus, Soy, and Herb Cedar-Plank-Grilled Salmon, 104, *105*
Sockeye Salmon Thai Red Curry with Chili Crisp, *158*, 159
Tinned Salmon Carbonara with Arugula and Pine Nuts, *150*, 151
Tinned Salmon Niçoise Sandwich, 100, *101*
Wild Salmon Noodle Soup, *38*, *39*, 40
salt. *See* sea salt
sandwiches and toast
Fancy Toast with Homemade Ricotta and Salmon Caviar, *84*, 85–86, *87*
Fried Oyster Toast, 99
Halibut Burgers with Wild Chimichurri, *32*, 33–34
Smoked Salmon Scramble with Caper-Dill Cream on Toast, *8*, 9
Tinned Salmon Niçoise Sandwich, 100, *101*
sauces, spreads, and seasonings
Anchovy-Herb Butter, 98
Apple, Rhubarb, and Cranberry Chutney, 144
Avocado-Cilantro Crema, 153, *155*
Caper-Dill Cream, *8*, 9
Create Your Own Seasoning Blends, 161
Dipping Sauce, *228*, 229
Fancy Spring Butters, 17–18
Homemade Ricotta, *84*, 85–86, *87*
Honey-Cider Glaze, 147
Lemon-Dill Cream Sauce, 208
Lemony Cream Dressing, 91
Lime-Cilantro Dressing, *96*, 97
Make Your Own Sea Salt, 57
Maple Applesauce, 194
Tahini Dressing, *224*, 225
Whipped Goat Cheese, 196, *197*
Wild Chimichurri Sauce, 34
Sauna, Relax and Rejuvenate in, 198–199
Scallops with Honey-Cider Glaze, Pan-Seared, 147
sea salt
Lemon Rosemary Sea Salt, 161
Make Your Own Sea Salt, 57
Sea Urchin Uni Butter, 17
Seafood Boil, Alaska; and variations, 125, *126–127*
Seafood Charcuterie Board, *174*, 175
Seasoning Blends, Create Your Own, 161
seaweed
Cured Salmon with Cucumber and Seaweed Salad in Lemony Cream Dressing, *90*, 91–92
Dill Bullwhip Kelp Pickles, *14*, 15
Harvest Edible Seaweed, 88–89
Harvest Seaweed for Your Garden, 10–11
Miso Seaweed Butter, 18

shellfish
See also clams; crab; shrimp and prawns
Alaska Seafood Boil; and variations, 125, *126–127*
Fried Oyster Toast, 99
Grilled Oysters with Miso Seaweed Butter, *46*, 47
Mussels with Spring Onions, Sorrel, Cider, and Cream, *58*, 59
Oyster Stew, 226
Pan-Seared Scallops with Honey-Cider Glaze, 147
Sea Urchin Uni Butter, 17
Seafood Charcuterie Board, *174*, 175
Tinned Octopus, Avocado, and Tomato Salad with Lime-Cilantro Dressing, *96*, 97
shrimp and prawns
Alaska Seafood Boil; and variations, 125, *126–127*
Garlic-Butter Wild Alaska Spot Prawns with Stir-Fried Noodles, 164
Shrimp and Crab Gumbo, *214*, 215
Simple Syrup, Fireweed, 124
Smoothie, Nutty Cinnamon Banana, 188
soups and stews
Creamy Tomato Soup with Basil Pesto, 176, *177*
Make Fish Stock, *114*, 115
Oyster Stew, 226
Shrimp and Crab Gumbo, *214*, 215
Wild Salmon Noodle Soup, *38*, 39–40
Spot Prawns with Stir-Fried Noodles, Garlic-Butter Wild Alaska, 164
Spring Equinox Feast, *48*, 49–67, *50–51*
Sprouts in a Jar, Grow, 7
spruce tips
Forage Spruce Tips, 64, *65*
Spruce-Tip Ice Cream, *66*, 67
Stock, Make Fish, *114*, 115
Strata with Goat Cheese and Dill, Smoked Salmon, 190, *191*
Summer Solstice Feast, *120*, 121–129, *126–127*

T

Tacos with Avocado-Cilantro Crema and Pickled Onions, Grilled Halibut, 153–154, *155*
Tahini Dressing, *224*, 225
Tea, Make Your Own Herbal, 167
Thai Red Curry with Chili Crisp, Sockeye Salmon, *158*, 159
toast. *See* sandwiches and toast
Tomato Soup with Basil Pesto, Creamy, 176, *177*
traditions
Celebrate the First Fish, 79
Cook Fish over a Fire, *102*, 103
Create Your Own Seasoning Blends, 161
Dig for Clams, 36
Eat Wildflowers, 116
Forage Fiddleheads, *22*, 23
Forage Spruce Tips, 64, *65*
Forage Wild Mushrooms, 134–135
Gather Rose Hips, 162, *163*
Go Ice Fishing, 204–205
Grow Bulbs Indoors, 189
Grow Sprouts in a Jar, 7
Harvest and Dry Herbs, 152
Harvest Edible Seaweed, 88–89
Harvest Seaweed for Your Garden, 10–11
Harvest Wild Nettles, 26
Jig for a Halibut, *30*, 31
Learn the Basics of Canning, 140–143
Light Up the Night with Ice Lanterns, 195
Make Fish Jerky, 94
Make Fish Stock, *114*, 115
Make Salmon Caviar, 80–81
Make Winter Bird Garlands, 211
Make Your Own Herbal Tea, 167
Make Your Own Sea Salt, 57
Pick Wild Berries, *72*, 73
Plant an Herb Garden, 16
Pour Homemade Candles, 216–217
Preserve Your Catch, 156–157
Press Flowers, 113
Quick Pickle Your Garden Vegetables, 148–149
Relax and Rejuvenate in the Sauna, 198–199
Share Your Harvest with Your Community, 107
Stock Your Pantry with Staples, 192–193
Tap a Birch Tree, 42
Tree, Tap a Birch, 42

W

Winter Solstice Feast, *220*, 221–231, *234–235*

STANLEY K
FALSE PASS
SK

Conversions

VOLUME

UNITED STATES	METRIC	IMPERIAL
¼ tsp.	1.25 mL	
½ tsp.	2.5 mL	
1 tsp.	5 mL	
½ Tbsp.	7.5 mL	
1 Tbsp.	15 mL	
⅛ c.	30 mL	1 fl. oz.
¼ c.	60 mL	2 fl. oz.
⅓ c.	80 mL	2.5 fl. oz.
½ c.	120 mL	4 fl. oz.
1 c.	230 mL	8 fl. oz.
2 c. (1 pt.)	460 mL	16 fl. oz.
1 qt.	1 L	32 fl. oz.

LENGTH

UNITED STATES	METRIC
⅛ in.	3 mm
¼ in.	6 mm
½ in.	1.25 cm
1 in.	2.5 cm
1 ft.	30 cm

WEIGHT

AVOIRDUPOIS	METRIC
¼ oz.	7 g
½ oz.	15 g
1 oz.	30 g
2 oz.	60 g
3 oz.	90 g
4 oz.	115 g
5 oz.	150 g
6 oz.	175 g
7 oz.	200 g
8 oz. (½ lb.)	225 g
9 oz.	250 g
10 oz.	300 g
11 oz.	325 g
12 oz.	350 g
13 oz.	375 g
14 oz.	400 g
15 oz.	425 g
16 oz. (1 lb.)	450 g
1½ lb.	750 g
2 lb.	900 g
2¼ lb.	1 kg
3 lb.	1.4 kg
4 lb.	1.8 kg

TEMPERATURE

OVEN MARK	FAHRENHEIT	CELSIUS	GAS
Very cool	250–275	120–135	½–1
Cool	300	150	2
Warm	325	165	3
Moderate	350	175	4
Moderately hot	375	190	5
Fairly hot	400	200	6
Hot	425	220	7
Very hot	450	230	8
Very hot	475	245	9

For ease of use, conversions have been rounded.

ACADIAN
XTRATUF

About the Authors

Claire (left) and Emma (right) are sisters, fishermen, and cofounders of the company Salmon Sisters. They grew up on a homestead in the remote Aleutian Islands and work as harvesters of wild Alaska seafood with their family. They are also authors of *The Salmon Sisters: Feasting, Fishing, and Living in Alaska*.

Their company, Salmon Sisters, celebrates coastal heritage, shares stories behind Alaska's wild seafood, and strives to strengthen ocean stewardship through quality products and design. Emma, who studied art at Williams College and design at the University of Washington, is the creative force behind the company; Claire, who studied at the University of Vermont, is all business. Emma and Claire reside in Homer, Alaska, with their families.

Learn more about Salmon Sisters at SalmonSisters.com and visit their Fish Shop and Flagship Shop in Homer, Alaska, during the summer season.

Printed in China

SASQUATCH BOOKS with colophon is a registered trademark of Penguin Random House LLC

27 26 25 24 23   9 8 7 6 5 4 3 2 1

Editor: Jen Worick
Production editor: Isabella Hardie
Designer: Anna Goldstein
Illustrator: Emma Teal Laukitis
Photography: Dawn Heumann, Brian Grobleski (pages 8,84,87,101,110, 150,158,197,201,202) and Evgenia Arbugaeva (pages 184-186)

Library of Congress Cataloging-in-Publication Data
Names: Laukitis, Emma Teal, author. | Neaton, Claire, author. | Heumann, Dawn, photographer.
Title: The salmon sisters: harvest & heritage : seasonal recipes and traditions that celebrate the Alaskan spirit / by Emma Teal Laukitis & Claire Neaton ; photography by Dawn Heumann.
Description: Seattle, WA: Sasquatch Books, [2023] | Includes index.
Identifiers: LCCN 2022055875 (print) | LCCN 2022055876 (ebook) | ISBN 9781632174338 (hardcover) | ISBN 9781632174345 (epub)
Subjects: LCSH: Seasonal cooking. | Cooking, Alaska. | LCGFT: Cookbooks.
Classification: LCC TX714 .L377 2023 (print) | LCC TX714 (ebook) | DDC 641.5/64--dc23/eng/20221202
LC record available at https://lccn.loc.gov/2022055875
LC ebook record available at https://lccn.loc.gov/2022055876

ISBN: 978-1-63217-433-8

Sasquatch Books
1325 Fourth Avenue, Suite 1025
Seattle, WA 98101

SasquatchBooks.com

RUNDENS